T0064295

After Roll Call

A STATE TROOPER'S MEMOIR

TOM VERGE

iUniverse LLC
Bloomington

AFTER ROLL CALL
A STATE TROOPER'S MEMOIR

Copyright © 2014 Tom Verge.

All rights reserved. No part of this book may be used or reproduced by any means, graphic, electronic, or mechanical, including photocopying, recording, taping or by any information storage retrieval system without the written permission of the publisher except in the case of brief quotations embodied in critical articles and reviews.

iUniverse books may be ordered through booksellers or by contacting:

iUniverse
1663 Liberty Drive
Bloomington, IN 47403
www.iuniverse.com
1-800-Authors (1-800-288-4677)

Because of the dynamic nature of the Internet, any web addresses or links contained in this book may have changed since publication and may no longer be valid. The views expressed in this work are solely those of the author and do not necessarily reflect the views of the publisher, and the publisher hereby disclaims any responsibility for them.

Any people depicted in stock imagery provided by Thinkstock are models, and such images are being used for illustrative purposes only. Certain stock imagery © Thinkstock.

ISBN: 978-1-4917-3360-8 (sc)
ISBN: 978-1-4917-3361-5 (e)

Library of Congress Control Number: 2014907791

Printed in the United States of America.

iUniverse rev. date: 5/14/2014

Contents

Dedication..vii

Preface ix

Introduction..xi

Part I   Troop H, Leon County, Tallahassee 1

Part II   Troop D, Brevard County District, Cocoa ... 18

Part III Troop A, Escambia County District,
          Pensacola 72

Part IV Epilogue 116

About the Author... 123

Dedication

I dedicate this book to all the troopers who have given their lives trying to keep the citizens of the State of Florida safe on the highways; to my wife, Vera, who understands me; and to my grandchildren, who never knew me when I was a Florida Highway Patrol trooper.

Dedication

Preface

When a state trooper puts on his or her uniform and walks out the door, they don't know whether this may be their last trip from home. They often find themselves in circumstances that are much bigger than they are and have to find a way to deal with the situation—and generally do it right. They may be called on to deal with the pulpwood hauler or leaders of our state or nation.

A trooper sees things regularly that would turn the stomachs of ordinary citizens. He or she has to console people as a chaplain, or may have to take a life. They may be called on to help pick up unmentionable things after a tragic accident. The odd shifts and call outs in the middle of the night; or suddenly being called away from home for an extended period of time have cost many a trooper their family. But through it all, they head out the door at the next hour of a new shift.

In order to cope with all the tragedy that they see and deal with on a daily basis, they develop a very thick skin so very little emotion is revealed. They have a gallows sense of humor that ordinary citizens would not understand. They laugh with their fellow officers and cry alone. They release stress by developing close relationships with other troopers. They help them through the bad times and play jokes on each other during the slow times.

Troopers tell each other stories of the odd situations they have handled or, maybe, brought on themselves. These are seldom written in a report but talked about during their coffee breaks and hardly ever shared with anyone else. In order to keep these stories from being lost, I began writing them down for my grandchildren, who never knew me as a state trooper, since they were born after I retired. As the text grew into what it is today, other retired troopers, friends, acquaintances, and family members kept saying, "I want a copy." That's when I decided to put the stories into a book.

Although I have been retired twenty-three years, I am proud that I can still call these men and women, those that have gone on and those that are still protecting the highways and roads of Florida, my brothers and sisters. I thank each and every one of them for the job they are doing.

Introduction

In the mid-1960s and through the early 1970s, the United States was in an upheaval due to the Vietnam War. There were protests against the war as well as race riots. Cultural changes were taking place throughout the country. Great strides were being made in our space program based on the challenge made by President John Kennedy in May 1961 to place a man on the moon in ten years.

With these events as a backdrop, I became a Florida Highway Patrol trooper on November 15, 1967. Florida was the location of the Apollo space program, the 1972 Republican and Democratic conventions, racial tension, and continuing Cuban problems, including the Mariel Boat Lift of 1980. I was involved in all these events, while at the same time developing my law enforcement skills to become efficient, dependable, and worthy of being called a state trooper.

Introduction

PART I:

Troop H, Leon County, Tallahassee

November 1967–July 1969

On November 15, 1967, I became a Florida Highway Patrol trooper. I had applied in June 1967, just a few days after being separated from the navy in Pensacola, Florida, where I lived from 1964 to 1967. Four months would go by before I would hear anything further from the highway patrol. In October I received a letter from the FHP, inviting me to Tallahassee, where I joined forty-nine other applicants for two days of testing, a physical, and several interviews. Two weeks later I received a letter stating that I had been hired and was to report to Tallahassee.

My first assignment was Troop H, Leon County, Tallahassee. This duty station was nearly impossible duty for a rookie trooper to get as a first assignment in 1967. Since almost every new trooper had to go through Miami before being assigned anywhere else in Florida, everyone in Tallahassee thought I knew someone or was related to someone. I found out later that the FHP didn't do me any favors assigning me to Tallahassee.

One of my sons was scheduled for surgery the same day I was to report, so Lieutenant Joe Collins, who was

1

the acting troop commander of Troop H in Tallahassee, allowed me to start a day early for orientation in order to be at the hospital with my wife, Vera, and son during the surgery. That act of kindness by Lieutenant Joe Collins was probably the only nice thing he ever did for me.

The FHP paid by the month; since I had started working in the middle of November, on December 1, I received a fifteen-day paycheck. This had to last us through the entire month of December. Thank goodness Vera had the forethought to have purchased some toys for our sons while we were still in the navy. That turned out to be their Christmas gifts while, of course, we did without. There was also the possibility of running out of food before the end of the month, so we occasionally got help of some kind from one of the other troopers who knew about our plight.

The first month as a state trooper I wore civilian clothes and spent a lot of time in the radio room, learning how things were done from that prospective. The first time I rode in a patrol car I got carsick. I think it was nerves, but it was several months before I was able to live that down. The rest of my time was spent riding with a field training officer, usually a senior trooper.

I quickly found out that Lieutenant Collins didn't think rookie troopers should ever be assigned to such a plum location as Tallahassee. His idea, along with those of most supervisors, was that all new troopers should go to the south Florida districts, as he did, where there was tons of work and a new trooper could learn his craft. He proceeded to make my life miserable for the short time I was in Tallahassee.

One morning I was working a county road where we had been alerted about speeding cars. From where I was sitting, I saw a flock of wild turkeys crossing the road at about the same time as an oncoming vehicle. The car clipped the last gobbler and knocked it into the grass on the shoulder. The car never slowed, so after he was gone, I went over and saw the turkey still flopping around. I quickly finished it off, put it in the trunk, and headed home. I thought I had a real prize. Vera spent the day dressing the turkey and cooking it. The thing was so tough and smelled really wild—to the point that not only could we not eat it, but neither would the dog or cat. I still am reminded of that by Vera once in a while.

Trooper Bobby Burkett was assigned as my field training officer. I learned a great deal from Bobby, who later on became the director of the Florida Highway Patrol. I could always tell when Bobby was having an off day. He would have me fill out the accident reports while investigating accidents and later take the field copy home and write a neat copy to be turned in at the station. It was not unusual for me to sit all evening filling out reports after a nine-hour shift—that would be the original and two carbon copies since there were no copy machines available in 1967. Sometimes if I was tired or in a hurry, I would forget to turn the carbon paper, mess up the report, and have to start over. To make things worse, I would have what I thought was a perfect report and give it to Bobby at the beginning of the next shift. He would take one look at it and then tear it up, saying that it was the worst report he had ever seen. He'd hand me the pieces and tell me to redo it. It took only a few of those to realize that we were still filing reports under his name, and he was a good trooper who would only accept the best out of me since a lot of people would be seeing them.

I realized pretty quickly that I was working with some of the real legends of the patrol: Jim Hanks, Ed Glenn, Red Murphy, Lance Bowen, Tommy Fifer, Melvin Lee Galloway, and a few others. I heard many of their stories when we would get together at coffee breaks. These were the type of troopers that had stories told about them all over the state.

Tallahassee is the capital of Florida and home of the highway patrol general headquarters, both of which bring their own set of problems to the doorstep of a new trooper. Contrary to popular belief, there are people that are immune to traffic enforcement. One of my problems was that I had to figure out not only that bit of information but also who was exempt. On the one hand, I wanted to let the powers in the FHP know that I was indeed learning my craft. At the same time, I was supposed to be selective as to who got the tickets.

Lieutenant Collins was always looking for something to ding me about, or so it seemed. One incident involved my (now late) brother, Al, who was down visiting us. I had Al riding with me so that I could show him what I did for a living. When the lieutenant requested I go to the office that morning, I had a feeling that he was up to something. I was getting gun-shy any time I got a call to go to the office. On the way to the office, I dropped Al at a gas station down the road a ways. The first thing Lieutenant Collins did was look in my car and ask where my passenger was. I truthfully was able to tell him that I had dropped my passenger off at a gas station.

Another time, I called in sick with a fever. On the way home from the doctor's office, we stopped at a hardware store for something and ran into Lieutenant Collins. A few days later he called me to the office and told me he thought I had lied about being sick. From then on I had to get a note from the doctor to prove I had really been sick. That was my life while I was in Tallahassee.

In January 1968 there were 791 troopers in Florida. They assigned radio identification numbers by seniority, and of course mine was 791. As the highway patrol grew in numbers, it became easier to tell senior troopers from younger ones. In the late sixties we were small enough that I met and knew most of the troopers. Over the years we either served on many details together or I went to refresher schools with them. However, by the mid-1970s the ID numbers reached into four digits, as there were many more troopers.

Troopers, like shipmates in the navy, rely a great deal on the man next to them. In our case it was our zone partners, or the trooper in the next area, as he was the only one to help you when things hit the fan. He was also the one that either was the butt of a practical joke or helped you pull one on another trooper.

Three months after I started as a trooper, I found myself on the midnight shift. I was the only trooper in about five counties most nights. I worked crashes in all eight counties of the troop at one time or another. The counties with smaller populations did not always have a trooper working after midnight, and on those nights I took every call.

One night I was directed by the dispatcher to head out State Road 20, west of town. There I was to look for a supposed UFO that had landed in the middle of the highway. As I traveled out toward whatever was blocking the road, I began to recall movies of the poor old policeman knocking on the door of a spaceship and being vaporized by a ray gun. I made it about ten miles west of town, pulled over, exited the car, and stood on the hood, so that I could see farther west. I reported back that I couldn't see anything and headed east, back toward town. Just so you know, I wasn't afraid. I just didn't feel like being zapped with a ray gun.

One evening I was on this same stretch of road and spotted a drunk driver. When I stopped him, I saw that he was much bigger than me, and there was no such thing as a backup in 1968 in Leon County. There was no one but me on the midnight shift. The drunk driver was not unfriendly, but he did not want to go to jail. I put the cuff on one arm and it clicked once—he was that big. He kept the other arm stiff so that I couldn't put the second cuff on it. Finally, in exasperation, I pushed him off balance and put the second cuff around the door handle.

I then told the drunk, "You are going to jail. Now, you can either ride or walk—your choice." I got in the car, rolled down the passenger window, and started the engine. I said, "If you want to ride, get in." Because I had locked the door with the cuffs, he couldn't get in. I made him climb in the window and ride to the jail folded up in the passenger seat. He did go to jail.

In April 1968, five months after I became a state trooper, Martin Luther King Jr. was shot and killed in Memphis, Tennessee. Places all over the country erupted into race riots, including Tallahassee. The center of the trouble for Tallahassee was on the Florida A&M University campus. The city of Tallahassee called and requested help from the FHP, especially around the capital office buildings. I was called into work and was assigned the intersection of East Gaines Street and South Calhoun Street. The city had dumped a load of dirt in the intersection as a barricade. I was there with another trooper and two city policemen. As the afternoon turned to evening, we occasionally heard gunshots and word came to us that the students had obtained a rifle.

We used the dirt pile as a place to hide behind. Later, after dark, city trucks came back and removed the street light at the intersection. The students we were facing finally obtained a bow and arrows after the gunshots stopped. Sitting behind a pile of dirt and suddenly seeing an arrow sticking into the front of the pile made us reconsider where we should be posted. We did move back into deep shadows, and the first shots were the only ones to come close to our position. I think the plan we had was to just surround the area and let the students vent until they tired out. We stayed on our post until our replacements showed up a little after midnight. The only occurrence of damage reported was that the students had torn up their own campus.

I stayed in Tallahassee twenty-one months. Some of them were good months and some not so good. Lieutenant Collins refused to allow me to go to the FHP Academy

7

for fourteen months. I was a seasoned trooper before I did go in January 1969. The academy was stricter in those days than they are nearly fifty years later. When I went, I was restricted to the academy, even though I lived in town. I could go home Saturdays but had to return to the building for roll call by midnight. I could leave again Sunday morning and had to return by 9:00 p.m. Sunday night. Today's recruits are off after class until classes start the next day.

I learned that Florida is indeed a small state when it comes to knowing troopers. My roommate in the FHP Academy was Chuck Williams out of Jacksonville. Over the course of the three months we were living together, I learned a lot about Chuck and Jacksonville. He was stationed with a trooper by the name of Marty McIntire. Marty and his brother Andy were from Pensacola, where their dad owned an ambulance service, and I had known them from my navy days.

Andy and Marty had joined the FHP, and Marty was assigned to Jacksonville. He was involved in an accident that caused disabling injuries and had to leave the FHP shortly after the accident. Andy served a few years and quit to take a job with a Tallahassee trucking company. Chuck also knew another trooper from Jacksonville that I had met when I first tested for the FHP in 1967, Charlie Ragsdale. Ragsdale was also from Pensacola and would eventually be stationed in Brevard County with me, and again in Pensacola.

Our class was declared the thirty-fifth recruit training class and had about forty students from all over Florida. We made friends there that would go on to become the new leaders of the department, field supervisors, and well-respected traffic homicide investigators.

Years later I met up with several active troopers at a troop fish fry. We were discussing how things had changed over the years. We then began to discuss what class we were in at the academy. The answers varied from class 98 to class 106. When it was my turn, I said that I was in the class 35. One of the young troopers looked at me and said, "Oh, you're one of those in the black and white pictures, aren't you?" The comment made me feel very old suddenly.

I never got a weekend off while I was in Tallahassee. My days off were either Mondays and Tuesdays or Wednesdays and Thursdays. That worked out to our advantage because Vera and I would take the kids and go somewhere on those days. If we went to a park, we usually had the place to ourselves. We roamed the back roads of the area, looked at sink holes I had discovered while I was working, or traveled to Thomasville, Georgia, which was just up the road. I was able to help Vera with the boys and we all enjoyed the outings. Our first spring there, the owner of the trailer park where we lived invited us to spend the day at his plantation. We not only roamed the plantation for the day, but we were allowed to pick peaches from the orchard. That was a real treat.

Vera and I discovered that just because a patrol car sat in our driveway, some members of the general public thought I was on duty. One day after one of our excursions, we came home to find that a person had been inside our house and had used our kids' crayons and a tablet to write us a note asking for help. The person had left an address. Being a new trooper, I went and saw that the address was for a shack in the woods. I contacted the proper organizations to give the woman the food and assistance she needed. Needless to say, after that incident we made sure the doors were locked on our house when we were gone.

We often took the boys to McClay Gardens State Park, north of Tallahassee. There was a lake with a beach and grills. Most of the time we had the beach to ourselves. We always cooked hot dogs and other fixin's. It was a good time to be a family.

One time when we were at the state park, I noticed another family down the beach looking for a child. One of the family members located the child in the lake and not breathing. I started easing their direction, watching what they would do. The man who held the child started beating it on the back to no avail. I rushed up, grabbed the child, who by then was starting to turn blue, and started a new technique we had recently learned in the navy called mouth-to-mouth resuscitation. Within a couple of minutes I had the boy breathing. In the meantime someone had called an ambulance and the family left, following the ambulance to the hospital.

I never did find out the child's name or the family name. I was told later by one of the park rangers that the child had survived and would have no lasting effects. The same ranger gave me a lifetime pass to McClay Gardens for saving the boy's life. I was also selected as a nominee for state trooper of the year as a result. A couple of other troopers received the award that year for climbing into a cave and rescuing someone. What an honor just to be recognized like that, and me with less than a year on the FHP.

I received several complimentary letters from people that I had assisted in one way or another while I was in Tallahassee. However, I received several complaint letters as well. The good ones we called "atta boys" and the bad ones were called "aw s★★★" letters. One aw s★★★ could wipe out all the atta boys you got.

One morning I was traveling the truck route around Tallahassee and saw a wildfire sweeping down on a wood-frame house in the middle of a field. I saw a woman standing on the porch, watching the fire approach her home. Without thinking, I turned into the driveway to the house and discovered not one but two old women still in the house. I grabbed them both, placed them in my car, and raced ahead of the fire, back to the highway, where I called for the fire department. By the time they got there, the house was engulfed in flames. I received a letter of commendation for saving the two women from the burning house. I never considered what I did as heroic. Later, a son of one of the women came out to thank me for saving his mother's and aunts' lives that day. It was just something I did, never expecting any thanks or recognition for doing it.

One of the benefits troopers had in Tallahassee was that we did volunteer work at the Florida State University Doak Campbell Stadium, directing traffic and security at the stadium before and during games. I became a Seminole fan from that point on. Doak Campbell Stadium in 1968 held about fifteen thousand people, and Bill Peterson was the coach. I met Ron Sellers, Kim Hammond, Fred

Biletnikoff, and several more Seminole players who went on to stellar careers in pro football. They always treated the security as one of their own. I managed to see several games that year, especially when I had the midnight shift. Lose a little sleep and see a game—cool.

In 1968, our ticket books had carbon paper between each of the five copies of each citation, and we had to account for every copy. One day I was assigned to assist with aerial traffic enforcement out on US Route 90 near the Leon/Jefferson County line. The idea was that the pilot would clock the target vehicle through a measured quarter mile and call down the speed and description of the vehicle. This particular day he called down the speed and description, but before the vehicle got to our location, the driver made a U-turn, attempting to elude us. Since it was my turn, I raced to my car, forgetting that I had left my ticket book on the trunk lid. When I spun around to take up the chase, I flipped my ticket book into a nearby creek. Needless to say, the chase was over since I had to retrieve my book. Pages and carbon were everywhere, so into the creek I went after taking off my shoes and gun belt. I think I got everything back eventually, even though I couldn't read any of the pages.

We had a character in Tallahassee named Harry Culberson Jr. who thought of himself as a trooper wannabe. He had been authorized by general headquarters to have blue lights and a siren in his personal vehicle. He also had a scanner, so he knew when we were responding to an accident with injuries. One night I got the call for an accident with injuries on the Centerville Road. As I rounded a curve, there was Harry's car lying almost on its side in the ditch. I stopped, looking for Harry, who was nowhere to be seen. As I looked in the vehicle, there was Harry still in the front seat. He had been wearing his seatbelt but had fallen out of the driver's seat and was too far away to reach the belt latch. I was laughing so hard it was difficult for me to unfasten him. Several years later I found out that other troopers I would work with in other locations had several tales to tell about Harry Culberson Jr.

Occasionally I patrolled one of the local highways and would give chase to a speeding car only to learn that it was a trooper in an unmarked car passing through. We had no interstates or any devices to assist us detecting speeders in those days. You had to wait until the speeder was past you, almost out of sight, make a U-turn, and then pace them until you were satisfied you knew how fast they were going. It would sometimes take miles to catch them and pace them before they were actually stopped. One trooper out of the Panama City office, Sergeant Cal Weston, was one that I seemed to chase all the time. He eventually started calling me on the radio when he got close to Leon County, with an offer to buy coffee.

Another trooper I met on the midnight shift was Trooper Ken Halsey, also out of the Panama City office. I saw him one night in Leon County, when I didn't know anyone else was supposed to be out, so I called him. We met for coffee and he told me who he was and where he was stationed. I remember telling him he was a ways out of his area since Panama City was one hundred miles west of Tallahassee.

He said, "Well, my car has State Trooper on the side of it, and I'm still in Florida as far as I can tell." I met him several more times, and not always in Tallahassee.

I used to watch an intersection on the south side of Tallahassee where we investigated a lot of accidents. It was called Four Points locally and was where two highways crossed in an X rather than a standard crossing intersection. People would run the stop signs there and cause accidents. One evening I had pulled off the roadway next to a utility pole and was watching traffic. I saw a car run the stop sign, and as I was pulling out in pursuit, I scraped a guide wire on the pole. It tore a hole in the right side of my car. Not knowing how to handle this incident, I called a senior trooper. After telling him what I had done, he told me to go to a certain garage in town, where he would meet me. The owner was there when I arrived and told me to leave my car at the end of my shift and he would take care of everything. I did as instructed, and the next day when I went to get my car, there was no evidence that an accident had ever occurred. That was the first and only time I did that, and I still feel guilty about it.

I worked several unusual accidents while in Leon County. The most unusual was one where a car had struck a bridge abutment while traveling west on US Route 90. This was before there were interstate highways. The FHP traffic homicide investigator had been called, and I was trying to finish my part of the investigation. As a part of the report, I had to list the coordinates for the exact location on the highway where the accident occurred. I checked my straight line map and couldn't locate the numbers I needed. Something didn't look right;

I called the homicide investigator. Together we discovered that there was a very small corner of the county where the highway left Leon County and reentered Jefferson County for a short distance, with the end of the bridge being the county line. The accident was then reassigned to Jefferson County. The car had actually hit the county line and killed the two occupants.

Vera and I finally decided to buy a house and get rid of our mobile home. We had been in Tallahassee about eighteen months and were getting settled in. After a search of the area, we found the house we wanted. The builder/owner allowed us to move in and pay rent until the closing date. Unknown to us at the time, three months later we would be transferring.

The dislike Lieutenant Collins had for me eventually boiled over to a point where he said that he was looking for any way he could to get me fired. This conversation took place after an incident that occurred where I found a stray, dirty, wet poodle while I was traveling across town one afternoon. I picked up the dog and took it to a local vet I used for my own dog. Sometime later the dog died, and I suppose, like any vet, this one did not lay the dog out and wait for the owner to show up. Instead, he took it out to a shed and stored it with other dead animals waiting for the crematorium van to haul it away. That was where the owner found the dog. He was told that an FHP trooper had brought it in. Of course they called the local FHP station and found out that the trooper was me. Lieutenant Collins called me in, and in the course of the investigation he told me he thought I was trying to steal the dog. He also thought I should buy the owners another dog. I refused to do that. He had the first sergeant stand outside his door, listening, and when the lieutenant finished the interview, he had me see the first sergeant, who asked me the same questions.

After that incident I felt that I could no longer work for someone who thought I was a thief and a liar, so I went to Trooper Hugh Lewis, whom I respected, for some advice. He was a trooper stationed at the governor's mansion. He was usually assigned the midnight shift and I would often slip by there to have coffee with him when I was on the same shift. We had discussed what was happening between Lieutenant Collins and me several times in the past. He suggested that I should ask for a transfer since I didn't have to stay in Tallahassee. He recommended that I try and get to Brevard County, where he had once been stationed. He had liked his time there and felt I would also. I put in for a transfer to Brevard County through Major Eldridge Beach, who was responsible for transfers of troopers statewide and worked at the general headquarters building.

It may sound like I am bitter about the way I thought I was treated while stationed in Tallahassee. But I was not the only trooper that was treated that way, and as the years went by, I found that it was a good learning experience for me. After that assignment I refused to let anyone else treat me the way Lieutenant Collins had, and the experience made me a better trooper. I knew I was a better person and trooper than what he saw in me, so I decided right then that I would prove it everywhere else I was stationed.

About the time we were notified of the closing on our new house, I received my transfer papers, which was for

July 15, 1969. We just had enough time to go to Brevard County, meet a couple of troopers, and locate a house. On the day we closed on the house in Tallahassee, we became homeowners in the morning and sold the house we had worked so hard to get that same afternoon. A week later we moved to Troop D, Brevard County, in the Melbourne District. We found a house in Rockledge.

Interestingly, I found that transferring out of Tallahassee, although disruptive for my family, was one of the best things I could have done. Tallahassee, first being the capital of Florida and second the location of the FHP general headquarters, caused a lot of problems for a young, new trooper trying to learn his craft while at the same time dealing with the politics of the area. I suppose that starting out a long way away from such an area would have been better for me in the long run, but I didn't have a choice. I was not about to tell those that hired me that Tallahassee was not a place I wanted to be stationed. When I arrived there, I wanted to put my best effort into the job, and I felt I was continually slapped down for trying to do just that.

PART II

Troop D, Brevard County District, Cocoa

July 1969–August 1974

Brevard County is the home of NASA Kennedy Space Center, located on Merritt Island, east of Titusville. I was assigned to the Cocoa area or Central Brevard County with eight other troopers. This area included all highways in and around Cocoa, Rockledge, Merritt Island, Cocoa Beach, and Cape Canaveral. The St. Johns River is the western boundary to Brevard County, and the county is the longest in Florida at seventy-two miles. It is about twenty-five miles wide with one-third of that width taken in by the St. Johns River basin. Cocoa is divided from Merritt Island by the Indian River. Merritt Island is split down the center by Sykes Creek, and the eastern boundary is the Banana River. Cocoa Beach and Cape Canaveral are located on the barrier island fronted by the Atlantic Ocean. The central territory of the FHP was from the Sharps Community on the north to the Eau Gallie Causeway on the south, and from the Atlantic Ocean to the county line.

My first day in Brevard County, July 15, 1969, I was assigned to ride with Trooper Don Shaw. Any time a trooper moves into a new area, he is assigned to a local trooper to learn the nuances of the area: court systems, highways, how to deal with paperwork with the nearest FHP office twenty-seven miles south, etc. However, at that time they were preparing for the launch of Apollo 11 on July 20, 1969. The FHP estimated there would be over one million people to witness the launch. Of course our job would be to move traffic and see that no roads were blocked.

The day of the launch I was in my own car, assigned to what was known at the time as the turn basin. The turn basin was where submarines turned around and was located between the toll booths on State Road 528 (Bennett Causeway) and the south gate of Patrick Air Force Base. This was a prime viewing area for rocket launches outside the property of Cape Canaveral since the location was straight up the Banana River to the Cape Kennedy launch site, eleven miles north. I think half of the million people were there. I recall the launch clearly, but mostly I remember all the people. Of course, as visible as we were, we stopped and visited with people every chance we got. Some people wanted my autograph and photo just to prove they had been in Florida— amazing.

Vera and I had found a home in Rockledge in a neighborhood where four other active troopers and one disabled trooper lived. I moved in next door to A. C. Jackson, one of the other local troopers.

The disabled trooper in the neighborhood was Ron Adams. Ron had been one of the twenty-five troopers hired at the same time I was back in 1967. At his start, Ron, like myself, was assigned with a senior trooper who acted as his mentor. He had to wear civilian clothes until he was sworn in and then he would be issued uniforms.

Ron was riding with his field training officer on the 3:00 p.m. to 11:00 p.m. shift when his field training officer decided to join a nighttime driver's license and equipment check on a local street in Merritt Island. Ron, still in civilian clothes, was struck by a car that had failed to stop for the officers who were standing in the middle of the road. He received several broken bones and his head hit the windshield and corner post windshield support.

Ron was taken to Wuesthoff Hospital in Rockledge and was airlifted to a hospital in Orlando in critical condition. He was not expected to live and had not yet been sworn in as a trooper when the accident occurred. The other troopers were concerned that he would not be covered by workers' compensation insurance unless he was a sworn officer. The story I was told was that several high-ranking FHP members were present at the Orlando hospital, and all swore that when the oath was read to him, Ron said, "I do."

I knew Ron until he passed away many years later, and I knew he did not recall anything that happened in or after the accident. He received full pay as a sworn FHP officer and never wore a uniform. After many years of rehab, he was able to complete college and receive a degree.

That was a forgotten story for all these years until I was reading an e-mail sent out from GHQ, asking if anyone knew a trooper by the name of Ron Adams. I immediately replied with the story about Ron and his accident. Based on the information I was able to provide, GHQ located Ron's records and was able to provide a trooper color guard at his funeral. He died forty-four years after the accident.

After this accident happened, the FHP changed the way they received new trainees. They no were longer allowed in a patrol car until they were sworn in and in uniform. Since that time, the FHP is also sending the new recruit troopers to the police academy first before assigning them a duty station. They are sworn in on completion of the academy, and then when they reach their duty station, they are assigned a field training officer.

Troopers are also no longer allowed to hold nighttime driver's license checks. Although, they do still hold nighttime DUI check points, they have plenty of safety devices in use to keep officers safe.

During my initial interview with the district commander, Lieutenant Len Bradley, the reason for my taking a transfer from a plum duty station like Tallahassee to Brevard County came up. He already knew that a large part of the problem had been the tickets I was always writing to the wrong people. He put me at ease by telling me I could write as many tickets as I wanted and to whom I wanted as long as they broke the law. For the next five and a half years I was either the top ticket writer or second in all of Troop D, which covered seven counties, including Orange County, Orlando. Roosevelt Slayton, a trooper in Orlando, was either ahead of me or just behind me on that list.

My first midnight shift came in August, fifteen days after I arrived in Cocoa. As a way of greeting and learning how life would be in Brevard County, I was called to meet my field supervisor, a corporal, one night. I pulled in next to him and was listening to what he had to say when a tremendous explosion occurred under my car. It scared the stew out of me; it was so loud! The corporal said, "Welcome to Brevard County." That's when I found out that while one corporal was talking to me, another one slipped up behind and stuck a cherry bomb under my car. I like to tell my friends that during that time we felt like kids who had fast cars, carried guns, and had no adult supervision.

There was always a place and time for having a good time, but we were also the law enforcement on Merritt Island, a rather large area of about thirty-five thousand to fifty thousand people. The sheriff's department took care of the domestic problems and we handled everything else.

Soon after arriving in Cocoa, I was working the day shift with Trooper Don Taylor. He got a call assigning him to a wreck with possible fatalities. We both headed out to the accident site on the Bennett Causeway, where I was going to assist with the traffic. When we arrived, we found there were three fatalities. Trooper Taylor, I found out later, couldn't stand the sight of all the blood and told me he would handle the traffic if I would work the wreck. This was a high-speed head-on collision at the top of the Banana River Drive overpass. As I recall there were no skid marks prior to the crash.

The victims were a father and two sons, who were vacationing in the Cape Canaveral area with other family members. I worked my portion of the accident, and then, as a part of my duties, I had to locate where the victims were staying and try to notify the next of kin. That's when I found out they were vacationing in Florida and had rented a cottage in Cape Canaveral. I stayed with the deceased's wife and third son until they contacted relatives and got them headed down to assist. What a mess Trooper Taylor left me to handle.

One day I met an FHP auxiliary officer named Russ France who would become my best friend in Cocoa. The FHPA had volunteers who would ride with troopers and assist with traffic and other assigned duties when asked. By riding with the troopers, this would free up another trooper who would otherwise have to stop what he was doing and give assistance. Russ rode with me just about all the time I was in central Brevard. I would go a little early on my shift, pick up Russ, and we would stop at the Dobbs House, a local eatery, for coffee and pie before starting our shift.

Russ and I would talk for hours about our military experiences. He had been in the Marine Corps in WWII fighting the Japanese in the Pacific. He retired a master sergeant with many decorations for valiant service. He said that on one island his unit was moving inland in a personnel carrier and he was riding on the edge with his legs dangling off the side. Suddenly they came under mortar attack. One mortar landed in the vehicle and killed everyone in his unit except him. He was blown off and into a pond of stagnate water. He couldn't move due to injuries he received, and as night fell, the Japanese moved back into that area his unit had taken before being wiped out. Russ said he lay in the water with only his nose sticking out all night until other marines retook the area the next day. After we became very close as friends, he told me that he would take a bullet for me if ever the need arose. As I said, we became very close.

One morning, Trooper Taylor, Russ, and I were at the Dobbs house. The owner, Randy Dobbs, had brought us an entire cherry pie with our coffee. About the time he set it on the table, we received a call regarding what was known locally as the WEZY report. The local radio station, WEZY, had worked out an arrangement where a working road trooper would give a live traffic report. That caused us to have to be on a main thoroughfare when the call came in. I took the call and on a live broadcast gave a complete and detailed traffic report on one of the main roads on Merritt Island. Of course I was at the Dobbs House in Cocoa Beach the whole time. As far as I know, this is the first time I ever told that story outside family and a few troopers.

I hadn't been in Cocoa very long when I had my first official accident in my patrol car. It was a minor accident, where I hit the rear of another car stopped at a stop sign. Not bad for a first accident, but the sad truth was, about two weeks later I had another one at the same intersection; again, I hit the rear of a stopped car. Both times I had anticipated that the driver would start moving when traffic had cleared enough for them to pull out— they didn't. After the second accident I was suspended one day without pay. That was pretty steep considering how much a trooper was being paid at the time. Ordinary citizens being cited were fined twenty-five dollars, but we never received citations; we were suspended. That got my attention real fast.

One day I was sent to work an accident at the Brevard/Orange County Line, at the St. Johns River Bridge. Upon arriving I found that an airboat had been struck by a car—strange. The facts were that the river was too high for boats to go under the highway, so the airboat driver turned up a canal parallel to the highway until he found a suitable place where he could cross it. He failed to look for other traffic and gunned his boat so it would skid across the pavement. However, he never made it across the roadway and was struck by a car. The airboat driver, of course, was killed. After this accident and the two I had caused a few days before, the other troopers started calling me Black Cloud, which is a nickname I still carry.

Other troopers in that area were also given nicknames. We had Snack Pack, Chicken Hawk, Soda Cracker, Teddy Bear, and myself, Black Cloud. One day while holding a driver's license check on North Tropical Trail, I heard Trooper Mark Tremont (Teddy Bear) calling me over the car radio. Back then we didn't have handheld communication devices, so in order to answer him, I had to return to my car. At the time I was checking the driver's license of a rather large woman driving a tiny sports car. When he called me a third time, in exasperation I said out loud, "Well, go ahead, Teddy Bear." Obviously the woman thought I was speaking to her because she reached out, grabbed her driver's license, and in a huffy voice said, "Well, okay!" and drove off.

Over the course of five and a half years in Cocoa, we saw many rocket launches, both announced and unannounced. Many of them were communication satellites being put in orbit. The Apollo space program was putting men on the moon, and I saw all the launches from Apollo 11 on, until they ended the Apollo program. But it was always all the people that I remember most. They came from everywhere to see the launches, especially the manned ones.

Once, Governor Lawton Chiles came down to watch from the NASA viewing area. Afterward, there was a parade down State Road A1A in the community of Cape Canaveral. I happened to have my usual area to patrol during the launch and was assigned somewhere along the parade route. During the parade one of our regular summer afternoon thunder showers began. As Governor Chiles, known as Walking Lawton, came by, I hurriedly gave him my raincoat.

He thanked me later for the use of the raincoat, when it was returned, and I thought that would be the end of the incident. A few weeks later I received a nice thank-you note from the governor, which in part stated, "Thanks for picking me up at the airport and taking me to the launch viewing area." The trooper that did pick him up at the airport must have received a nice note thanking him for the use of the raincoat. I still laugh about that when I run across the letter.

I was fortunate to live near the station manager of WEZY radio station. He invited me and another trooper to view a night launch of a Saturn V rocket. Since we were working days that month, it worked out so that we could go. We ended up in one of the underground bunkers just a couple of miles from the launch pad. That was really exciting when the biggest rocket in the world lit up. Everything around us shook, including the ground. It was really a powerful rocket.

It was the practice of Jim Rathman Chevrolet in Melbourne, Florida, to give each astronaut a new Chevrolet Corvette, one of which was given to Thomas Stafford, the command pilot of Apollo 10. Working the midnight shift one night, I noticed a car with the tail light out traveling north on State Road 3 in Merritt Island. When I stopped the car, to my surprise, I came face to face with Tom Stafford. Both of us being from Oklahoma, we talked for a short while about home before I released him with a warning about the tail light. Before he left he gave me photographs of Apollo 10, the command ship called Charlie Brown and the lunar module named Snoopy. There was also a photograph of the moon as they orbited it. He autographed each picture so I could give them to my sons. He was and remains a really nice man.

Another time I was working late evenings when I stopped a speeding car out by the St. Johns River. It turned out to be the driver of Robert Dole, who was a passenger in the car. This was not the first time he and I had crossed paths. When I was a kid of ten or twelve, we lived on Thirteenth Street in Independence, Kansas. My brother and I were playing outside after a rain, hiding in bushes and throwing mud balls at cars as they went by. One car stopped. We had an escape route planned and took it at a dead run. As we came in the back door of our house, someone was knocking on the front door. It turned out to be Robert Dole, who was upset about his car, naturally. Being the age my brother and I were, we never planned out the part where people would be upset about having their cars hit by mud balls.

We ended up having to wash the car and apologize, and then we got our britches tanned. It was a hard lesson, and here was Robert Dole fifteen or so years later. I introduced myself, reminded him of the mud ball incident, and let them go after issuing a citation for excessive speed. He didn't offer me an autograph.

One of the things I liked about central Florida was that they had the Grapefruit League, which meant baseball. We had the spring training camp of the Texas Rangers baseball team in Cocoa. I took the boys out to the games when I could because we got in for free. The boys sometimes came away with a baseball, but I don't recall ever getting one of those autographed.

I had a canoe built while we were in Cocoa and we purchased a pop-up camper. We went camping every chance we had. I taught the boys how to handle a canoe, which was neat since they were only five years old. We didn't have to go far to find water and a place to camp. My mom and dad came for a visit and we took them camping around central and south Florida. I still didn't get weekends off, so we had the same situation as in Tallahassee. The campgrounds were empty during the week for the most part.

Brevard County was so different from the northern part of Florida, which had hills and lots of oak trees, dogwoods, pines, and azaleas. Here the land was flat with palm trees, fruit trees, flowering trees, bushes, and lots of water. There were rivers, creeks, lakes, and the Atlantic Ocean. A Wyoming police officer named Jim

Olsen, who I had met while taking a law enforcement course at the University of North Florida in Jacksonville, asked me where all the rivers came from since we had no mountains. He was fascinated when I told him about all the underground springs that exist throughout Florida.

With all the water it was not unusual to see snakes and alligators sunning themselves on the edge of the highways. Such was the case when I saw an alligator about five feet long on the edge of the Bennett Causeway. Knowing the possible hazard of a motorist hitting the gator or it wandering into the road and causing an accident, I called for a wildlife officer. The call came back that they were all busy, and they asked if I could possibly remove it to a safe area myself. My zone partner that day was Trooper Joe Clayton. Joe came out to offer advice and some assistance. By this time we were attracting attention and a lineman in a phone truck stopped to offer his assistance. My friend Wayne from the local newspaper had heard about the gator on his police scanner and came out with a photographer.

The phone guy had some rope and a pole, so we decided to put the rope around its neck, tie it up, and drag it to a creek, where presumably it had come from. It sounded like a plan as we discussed it, but as we approached the gator, it decided we were intruding in its nap time and started after us. The phone guy, the newspaper guys, and I made it to the boundary fence and were sitting atop it before the gator left the road.

Eventually we, being smarter than the gator, roped it by surrounding it and managed to get it back to the creek as planned. There was a lot of laughing, and I made several friends that day. Joe, the phone guy, and I all got our picture in the paper for our efforts.

To show how invincible we thought we were, my friend Trooper Charlie Ragsdale and I often went fishing in the St. Johns River. We would start at the bridge at State Road 520 and fish the river flats for large-mouthed bass. We would wade the weed beds along the edge of the boating channel, fishing until we reached Lake Poinsett. Somehow we never thought of the possibility of alligators being nearby, especially since we strung anything we caught on our belts. Usually one or both of us would catch enough to have a fish fry at one of our houses.

On coffee breaks we often talked about anything but work. One such time the subject came up about Georgiana Cemetery on the southern end of Merritt Island. According to Don Taylor, one of my zone partners, it was supposed to be haunted. (Aren't all cemeteries?) I made the mistake of telling him that I didn't go to funerals or into cemeteries after dark.

Now, it hadn't been too long back that I had accidentally locked my keys in my car, a very embarrassing situation if you are a state trooper. The spare keys were stored in the first sergeant's office in Orlando, thirty-five miles away. Because of that I had an extra key made and kept it on my whistle chain. Not knowing this, my buddies concocted a reason, with the aid of the dispatcher, why I should be sent to Georgiana Cemetery one night.

These troopers had gone there first and were hiding when I arrived. I got out of the car and was looking for the reason I was sent there. I left the door open so I could hear the radio and the engine running since I was supposed to be the only one in the cemetery.

Suddenly the engine stopped and I was alone with just a flashlight and a patrol car with no keys in it. I saw my friends leave and immediately knew they had taken my keys. Rather than spend time looking for the keys in a haunted cemetery, I got out my spare key and drove off. I met them back in town where they were laughing at having left me stranded in the cemetery. I told them I had a spare key, and as far as I know, the lost keys are still in some remote part of that cemetery.

One night I was on the late shift and was working traffic on State Road 3, just south of the Bennett Causeway. As I was traveling north I saw an all-white apparition suddenly appear on the road in front of me. It floated across the road and disappeared on the other side. When I got to the area where I had seen it, I could not find any evidence of what it may have been.

Later I told my zone partner, Al Jackson, what I had seen and he busted out laughing. He took me back to where I had seen the object in question and showed me where the cement fence on each side of the highway overlapped. This caused an optical illusion, where it couldn't be seen on casual observation. As it turned out, there was a Catholic church located on the south side of State Road 3 and the nuns from the church lived on the north side of the highway. They would use the openings in the fences to get from the residence to the church for evening mass. When they crossed the road, from a distance they appeared to float. Another mystery solved and the name Black Cloud grew.

I usually had an FHP auxiliary member riding with me when I was working midnights. Al S., an auxiliary officer would ride with me on weekends. He would always end up asleep in the car. I discussed with him on several occasions that he needed to stay awake in order to know where we were at all times. This was in case there was an incident where I couldn't get to the radio for some reason; he could then call for backup and be able to tell where we were located.

The last night Al rode with me was a rainy night. Water collected on the edge of the pavement in puddles. I saw him asleep again so I ran the speed up to about eighty-five or ninety-five miles per hour and turned off my headlights. I started hitting those little puddles. It wasn't long before I saw his eyes open. He had heard the swishing of the tires hitting the puddles. He asked where we were, what we were doing, and why we were going so fast. Of course my response was we were just riding and going nowhere in particular. He thought about that for about a minute and asked me to take him home. I didn't say anything; I just slowed, turned around, and took him home. He never asked to ride with me again.

Our neighborhood had been built in an old orange grove, so in the springtime when the remaining trees bloomed, we were introduced to the sweet smell of orange blossoms. Not having smelled the sweet blossoms before, we often slept with the windows open and went to sleep inhaling that wonderful smell. I'll never forget living there because of the fruit trees.

I met the Crisafulli family, who owned Crisafulli Groves on North Courtenay Parkway in Merritt Island.

They asked if I could make a swing through their groves sometime during my shift as they had been losing a lot of fruit to thieves, especially trees along the local roadways. In return they offered me whatever fruit I wanted. This was not the proper thing to do, because I did not accept gifts for work as a state trooper. But I did tell them I would keep an eye out as I passed through the area.

Later I received a call from the station that a trooper from North Carolina wanted to ride with me on one of my evening shifts. Near the end of my shift he asked if there was anywhere he could get some fruit to take home with him. Recalling my conversation with the Crisafulli family, I took my new friend to the orange grove and pulled up to a full tree.

He asked if I had permission to get the fruit, but sensing a good joke, I told him no and he better start filling his grocery sack before we got caught. He took his shoes off, climbed on the top of my car and proceeded to fill his sack. He promised me that if I ever got to North Carolina, he knew an apple orchard where we could get all the apples I wanted. I love a good joke. He left for home thinking he had stolen the oranges.

Sometime during the first year I was stationed in Merritt Island, I worked a wreck involving an elderly man and his wife. Hans had torn up his car to the point that I had to give them a ride home. From then on for the next five years, Hans would see me and we would have to get coffee somewhere so he could tell me how much he liked the highway patrol. If he saw me working an accident, he would pull up and wait until I was finished and could talk. At Christmas time one year, he chased me down and wouldn't have it any other way but to give me a bottle of whiskey. It turned out to be genuine busthead whiskey—you know, the kind that gives you a really bad headache after one drink. But I had a friend in Hans until I transferred out several years later.

Around the summer of 1970, we started hearing about the Republican and Democratic conventions that were to be held in Miami. In anticipation of possible problems arising at those conventions, the highway patrol's riot squads began some intensive training. I was invited to be a member of the Troop D riot squad. This was a forerunner of swat teams. We traveled all over the state to practice riot techniques.

We were sent to Camp Blanding near Live Oak, Florida. Camp Blanding, an old WWII training base, used by the Florida National Guard. This was a three or four-day detail with squad-sized training and full-unit training. We also had firearms training. We practiced close order drill, which rotated into riot defense formations and single squad formations. Firearms training was with hand guns, which were standard issued sidearms, and 30 caliber carbines, which were also issued. On the twenty-five-meter course there was a competition, and at the end of the day, they named the top sixteen shooters in the state. I was fortunate enough to have made that list. Our team already had a sniper and heavy weapons specialists, so I joined the fire team as the shotgun protection.

The riot squad had its first test "under fire" when the Vietnam Veterans Against the War turned up in Gainesville at the University of Florida. The university called the local station asking for assistance, and selected troop squads, including Troop D, were called in to assist in putting down the disturbance.

An incident occurred during that riot where there was misconduct by a member of our squad. He was riding in my car at the time, so everyone in the car was implicated. The FBI investigated, and it was determined that I was not guilty of anything other than failing to stop the incident from occurring. I was not involved in the incident but was driving the car when it took place. As a result of the investigation, I was removed from the fire team and was reassigned as the tear gas specialist. The guilty trooper was disciplined and taken off the riot squad.

The riot squad continued to train using various sites. We were instructed to go to Winter Garden, Florida, for one session. The squad had obtained use of a borrow pit where we set up targets for practice with the various weapons we were to carry. I took plenty of gas canisters and shells for my practice. As I picked up the empty gas shells and canisters, I noticed that although spent, there was residue still in the shells. I went to my friend Tommy Thompson's patrol car and placed one of the expended teargas shells under his seat. Later we broke for lunch and loaded up and headed for town. We had traveled about three hundred feet when Tommy's car erupted with activity. Windows were opened and heads were sticking out of them all. Everyone had a big laugh at lunch, and Tommy had to leave the windows open during lunch to let the car air out.

After lunch we went back out for our afternoon session. Finally another trooper approached me and told me someone had put a snake in my car. I went over and indeed there was a rattlesnake coiled up in the front seat. I unlocked the door and decided that the best way to get the snake out was to quickly open the door, hook the snake with a handy item, and throw it out. I threw the door open, and as I did the snake jumped out and landed on my foot. Needless to say, I had a running fit. Tommy and his friends had killed the snake after lunch, gone into my car, and then tied monofilament fishing line to the snake and the door handle so that when I threw the door open, the dead snake jumped out of the car. Of course everyone on the squad was in on the joke and we all had another big laugh.

Several years later, after I was assigned to the Pensacola station, my friend Tommy Thompson became a sergeant and was working out of the Troop B St. Augustine station. He, along with a troop FHP pilot and another observer, was in one of the department planes looking for an escaped fugitive when the pilot made a fatal error. While turning, his plane made too sharp a turn and lost lift, causing the plane to fall from the sky, killing all three troopers aboard.

In 1987 while I was in Tallahassee doing some temporary work at GHQ and staying at the FHP Academy, I met several new recruits. They came to my quarters to visit and learn from a "seasoned trooper" about what to expect when they got on the road. In the course of the conversation, I told the story about the snake and the teargas. I noticed that one of the young troopers had tears in his eyes as I got along in the story. Afterward I asked what was wrong with the story that it made him cry. He replied that his name was Thompson and that he had grown up listening to that story from his dad. That made my day.

One of the supervisors for the riot squad was Corporal Bill Martin, who was also my shift supervisor. He acquired some land in Sharps, Florida, from the county and had us start building a shooting range with buildings and swinging targets. When the town we built became a training area, I practiced shooting gas grenades through windows and into open windows of cars. We knew we were training to head for Miami and kept our eyes on the news. I still had regular work to do and had a spot on the shift to cover, so I spent as much time as necessary to do both.

The lieutenant always wanted more citations; the sergeant and the corporals always wanted those of us that produced the most to write more. One time my zone partner, Joe Clayton, and I decided we could write a ton of citations for expired inspection stickers on cars along State Road 520. We just had to figure out a way to do it without getting run over, since Highway 520 was a four-lane highway with a paved median.

We finally worked out a plan where we would place one car in the median and one on the shoulder with the emergency lights on. This was supposed to slow down the traffic to fifty-five miles per hour, a point where we could see the inspection stickers and still have time to pull the violator over. I got my trusty friend Russ France from the auxiliary and Joe got another auxiliary man, and we put the plan into action. Over the next thirty days we probably wrote one hundred citations each for expired inspection stickers and expired tags.

Any time we were called away for other business, we would stop the operation. Then we would use random times to do it again. This was all on the day shift, of course, so at the shift change all operations ceased. One thing we failed to do was clear this traffic stop with the lieutenant. While we were on the traffic stop, he was getting complaints of troopers slowing traffic and causing people to be late for appointments and other various things. Our next stop was a meeting with him. Although he appreciated the increase in activity we were producing, he called a halt to our honey hole operation.

My sergeant, Ed Cranford, would sometimes have us help him with an old radar unit. This old unit was placed on a tripod, and the sergeant would call out the make and color of the target vehicle; we would chase it down and write a ticket to the driver. He would disguise what we were doing by pulling his spare tire out and raising his trunk lid. Our cars were yellow in the rear, so he had painted the inside of his trunk lid black. He did this until the lieutenant caught him and made him stop doing it.

About then was when we started using VASCAR. It was a computer mounted in the car, and we could clock cars traveling the same direction, either from the front or rear, or oncoming traffic, either in front or going away. Basically it was a computer that was a stopwatch, with the car measuring the distance and timing cars through the same measured distance. The trooper could measure a distance and sit on the side of the road and clock cars through the measured area.

Early one evening Trooper Don Shaw called me and wanted to know if I felt like running some VASCAR on newly opened I-95. He was already out there working, so I figured a good joke was in order. I knew where he was set up, so I headed north at a high rate of speed, knowing he was working the southbound traffic. As I passed his spot he called me to ask where I was. I gave him a location a couple of miles south of where I actually was, and he advised he would be back shortly, as he had clocked a violator northbound at a high rate of speed. Using my brake light cut-off switch, I made a hasty U-turn around a curve from Don. I passed him as he was headed north after a phantom car. I never did tell him it was me he had clocked.

One morning on the day shift I picked up Russ France and headed west toward I-95. There had been a muck fire in the nearby swamp and smoke was blowing across the interstate. There was a chance of fog moving into the area, so it was my mission to keep an eye on the interstate. By the time I got out there, fog had indeed moved into the area, and when it mixed with the smoke, it caused near-zero visibility. One of the Titusville troopers was working the north end of I-95 and had already called in several accidents due to the poor visibility. The decision was made to close that portion of the interstate, but we knew there were still cars already in the closed area, with many wrecks already being reported. I was sent into the fog to try and clear the road of damaged cars.

It was a harrowing experience, needless to say. I found the first of many accidents and got the people out of the cars. I'd parked my car in the grass near the fence and had the victims take refuge near my car. We had zero visibility and could only hear cars coming; then there was a crash and we knew it was another accident. I decided that Russ should walk up the shoulder as far as he could, keeping a safe distance from the roadway, to a point where he could at least hear cars coming. When he heard a car, he was to blow his whistle as a signal to me. I was in the road, trying to move the damaged cars onto the shoulder when Russ suddenly cut loose, blowing his whistle. As I ran for the fence, a big wind gusted and momentarily cleared the fog. There was Russ blowing his whistle at a large sign. He had heard a noise, thought it was a car on the northbound lanes, and with direction hard to determine, started blowing his whistle. I never let him live that down. But to his credit, he got my attention. At the end of the day we had over fifty cars involved in many different accidents before we could stop them from entering the fog.

We spent a lot of time off duty at Russ's home in Cocoa Beach. He had a pool and wanted us to help use it. He found out the boys didn't know how to swim, so he told Vera and I to leave the boys and stay home. He kept them several different days and had them swimming in no time.

One slow hot day after working an accident, Russ and I dropped by his house, and after moving his car out of the garage, I put my patrol car in where we would be able to hear the radio. He brought out swimsuits and quickly changed and took a cooling dip until the next call.

Once our entire shift got together, four troopers and their families, and had a fish fry at Russ's poolside. Later we went out in his boat to dip shrimp, or at least try. The method was to hang a light over the side of the boat to attract the shrimp and then dip them with a special shrimp net. With five of us in the boat, we expected to fill the boat. After a long wait, a lone shrimp came to the light. All of us slapped at it with the nets and somehow it panicked and started jumping. Russ was not dipping but handling the boat, so it came as a big surprise when the shrimp jumped into his shirt pocket. It turned out to be the only shrimp we caught all night.

Several evenings later Russ and I were traveling into the town of Cape Canaveral from the Bennett Causeway, and as I shined my spot light out across Banana River, all I could see was the red eyes of millions of shrimp.

Russ would occasionally ride with R. C. Smyth, one of the other troopers. R. C. had been married a couple of times before and decided to get married again. The wedding and party afterward was held at Russ and Jo's home in Cocoa Beach.

The newlyweds left for their honeymoon at about 10:00 p.m. in a rented motor home. The rest of us stayed with Russ, plotting what we could do to interrupt the wedding night. We had it figured out they would not go far in the motor home the first night, so we called the Melbourne station and had the Melbourne troopers search for where they had stopped. They located them parked under the Eau Gallie Bridge on the Satellite Beach side.

We all piled into Russ's motor home and headed out. After sneaking up on the parked RV, someone beat on the door, with all of us screeching.

R. C. suddenly appeared at the door in his tighty whities, carrying a dinner knife like it was a dagger and screamed, "I'll cut you!" We had a good laugh, built a campfire, and continued our party. We finished the party about 2:00 a.m. and decided to call it a night.

It may appear that all we did was play around and play jokes on each other, but you must remember that we investigated about thirty accidents each per month and wrote about five traffic citations per day. Plus we were always handling public relation details. I often transported blood and body parts in a relay from somewhere south of Cocoa to somewhere north of Cocoa. Those transports were frequently happening, and it took a lot of troopers to do them. We also had to work traffic details on scheduled manned and unmanned rockets both before and after a launch. There was always something going on, and the slow days were when we thought up unusual things to do.

We often had to appear in court, especially with working twenty-five to thirty crashes and writing over a hundred citations each month. From the time I joined the FHP in the late sixties, traffic citations were classified as misdemeanors and a person could be arrested and incarcerated for simply speeding. Just about every week we would have a fistful of subpoenas handed to us. That was just part of being a trooper. I didn't mind going to court but hated to lose a case that I knew to be a really good one.

One afternoon, on one of my days off, I was in Judge McLamore's court in the Cocoa Branch courthouse. I had to be a witness on a DUI case with lots of evidence and a high Breathalyzer reading. After hearing all the testimony, Judge McLamore found the violator not guilty.

When I left the courtroom, I let the door slam. As I was about to get in my car, I was met by two deputies who were the bailiffs for Judge McLamore. They told me the judge wanted to see me. I was escorted into his office where he met me.

What he told me that afternoon in his chamber, I used as my own credo the rest of my years on the FHP. He said first he did not like having to call me back into his office but that slamming the door to his courtroom was rude, disruptive, and unacceptable. I agreed with what he said and then told him that the case he dismissed was a righteous DUI arrest and I thought it should have gone in my favor.

He then said, "Listen to me, because I am only going to tell you this once. You will always be the arresting officer and I will always be the judge. It's your job to arrest people and they have a right to a trial. At that point you are just a witness, and since it is my courtroom, I can do whatever I want to—end of discussion. And don't ever slam the door to my courtroom again or you will be in more trouble that you can ever imagine." Needless to say, after that the tickets I wrote became just numbers and not much else. If the violators plead not guilty, I testified and left not caring any longer about the outcome of the case.

I was called to work a community fair on Fiske Boulevard in Cocoa one Saturday. I had my patrol car on display and answered thousands of kid's questions, and had that many more who sat in my car. I always liked community events for the public relations. The FHP had a good reputation in every community where I worked, and it was important to maintain the image those that came before me had created. At this event someone stopped by with a small child. A little girl had become separated from her family and was lost. A photographer took the picture as I questioned her. We found her parents and the picture, again, made the paper.

My next-door neighbor was Trooper Al Jackson. He was always trying to get his name in the paper. I never tried to do that, nor do I really want my picture or name in the paper. But I had made a friend while being chased by an angry alligator, and he saw that my name and picture were often in the paper. Al never could figure out how I managed to do that when he couldn't.

Another day Al Jackson, Sam Clark and myself were working the day shift in the central area. Not much was going on and we each had an auxiliary trooper with us, so we decided to hold a driver's license and equipment check on Sykes Creek Parkway. Rush hour was over and we could handle traffic without causing delays. In the middle of the check we noticed a flock of about eight or ten brown pelicans flying in single-file formation coming toward us. I guess Al had a premonition of pending doom, because he started running for his car. The rest of us watched him and were laughing. The pelicans swerved away from us and went toward Al for some reason. They flew over him before he reached his car, and of course one let go as he flew over and poop went streaming down across Al's hat and shirt. We were laughing so hard we had to get out of the road to keep from getting run over. I could have sworn the pelicans went after Al on purpose.

It was in late 1970 that I became a field training officer. New recruits from the academy who transferred into Cocoa were assigned to a veteran trooper for sixty to ninety days of on-the-job training. It was my job to mold the young troopers into someone who would carry on the traditions of the FHP and learn the craft. My first trainee was Recruit Trooper Marvin James. His first ID number was 1008, and he was the first trooper I had met with such a high number. Since he was my first trainee, I worked really hard with him. I tore up his reports the same way Bobby Burkett had torn up mine.

We were working the day shift one month when we received a call that a fast food restaurant had been robbed. We were given the description of the car and driver. Since we were only a few blocks away and I had just seen a city police car headed north on US Route 1, I decided we should head up Old Dixie Highway. We were stopped at State Road 520 when a vehicle somewhat matching the description turned east directly in front of us. I called in the tag, and the information came back that the car was suspected as the same one that had been involved in the robbery of a post office in Plymouth, Florida.

Marvin was driving and so I outlined how we would take the driver down. Marvin made the stop and we got the driver out. He did not match the description of the robber, but we interviewed him anyway. The described getaway vehicle had signs on each door and this vehicle didn't. Marvin consulted with me on what to do next. We decided to simply ask if we could open the trunk. The driver agreed, and inside we found the disguise he had been wearing, the magnetic signs he had taken off the doors, and the money he had stolen. It was a good takedown and the post office investigators wrote us both a nice letter for our files.

The highway patrolmen all drove Plymouth vehicles with big 440-cubic-inch engines. We used to turn the breather covers upside down to allow more air into the engine intake. With it upside down, they sounded like a jet engine when accelerating fast. They could be heard a block away. These were extremely fast cars and we did drive them that way once in a while. While the cars may have been fast, the brakes were terrible. Once you got up to a high rate of speed, it was hard to get the darn thing stopped.

My second trainee was Cliff Fields. Cliff had been a Pensacola city police officer who had always wanted to be a state trooper. I had help training him from Joe Clayton. Cliff was kind of wild, and I never knew if he got that from Joe or me or brought it with him from when he was a city policeman. I watched one evening when he and I were both called to a serious accident in the Sharps Community. I was trailing behind Cliff by about five hundred feet since it was not a good practice to follow close behind. (In that situation, a motorist may see and slow for the first emergency vehicle but not look for a second one. Lots of police car accidents occur because of that.) We had traveled about three or four miles and I noticed that Cliff was doing an unusually high amount of dodging other cars. He had also reduced his speed considerably. By the time we reached the accident site in Sharps, he could hardly stop his car. Those brakes we had on the cars would go away after slowing one or two times at a high rate of speed.

Cliff bought a boat so we could all go fishing on the St. Johns River. He and Joe Clayton were out on the river one day. He came to a *Y* in the river, and being indecisive,

Cliff failed to react in time and drove onto the island and completely out of the water. He went inland a ways and we had to get another boat out there to pull his back into the river. I think that was when Cliff sold the boat and bought a motorcycle. Go figure.

My third trainee in Cocoa was Mark Tremont. Mark was not inclined to get involved with the practical jokes I was always pulling and would go on to become a really fine trooper. His dad was a county judge in another county, and I think some of that rubbed off on Mark. Mark later went on to become a lieutenant colonel in our general headquarters in Tallahassee, but as a new recruit, he carried the nickname Teddy Bear.

I was assigned to traffic details at both car and motorcycle races at the Daytona International Speedway in Daytona Beach, Florida. The motorcycles races were interesting but not my cup of tea. What I recall about the car races was the noise the race cars made. Man, they were loud!

It didn't take long to figure out that whatever model of car won the race was the car that would speed on the highways after the race was over. Lots of citations were issued to those models. I took that knowledge back home with me, and every race thereafter, I would be out on I-95, listening to the races and waiting on the after-race traffic.

On another assignment to Daytona, I was sent to assist in testing Firestone tires. Firestone had come out with what they described as a pursuit tire that would stay together at the high speeds we were sometimes required to travel. We drove around the track at high speeds and the engineers examined them afterward.

We used the Firestone tires for about a year and then started having serious accidents involving the tires. I knew several troopers who were in pursuit and had serious accidents due to tread separation. Joe Clayton was involved in one such incident. He was traveling on the Bennett Causeway when one of the rear tires separated. The tread did not come completely off, just one end did. The loose end wrapped around the drive shaft and pulled the front end off the transmission. The drive shaft was still attached to the rear axle. The loose drive shaft beat a hole in the floorboard of the patrol car and vibrated all the knobs off everything in the car. Joe said that his hat was so far down on his head, he could hardly see. The loose tire tread meanwhile beat the quarter panel nearly off the rear of the car. Joe was lucky, as I knew one trooper who rolled his car several times and stopped rolling after it crashed against a tree. He had a broken leg that continued to cause him problems for many years afterward. The FHP went back to Goodyear tires after this series of accidents.

The FHP was also the point agency for some odd safety campaigns. One campaign named "Arrive Alive" was suggested and supported by Governor Rubin Askew. This included handing out ballpoint pens containing the "Arrive Alive" logo. With every citation issued, we were to have the violator sign with the pen and then give it to him. About 95% of the pens I handed out in this fashion were tossed out the window of the violator's car prior to leaving after they received the citation.

The FHP also set up traffic details for the "Arrive Alive" safety campaign. I went on one such detail to the Troop D Deland district and was assigned to the Daytona area. We were told to bring enough citation books so that the local supervisors did not have to issue any to out-of-town troopers. I took six books of twenty-five citations each and thought I had enough to last me the five days we would be there. I ran out after three days and called the local supervisor for more. He tried to get mad at me for not following their orders, but when he found out I had written 125 citations in three days, he changed his mind.

Our paychecks were barely enough to last from one month to the next. I discovered it was cheaper to have new heels put on a pair of shoes than to buy all new shoes. While I was waiting to have that done at a shoe repair shop in Merritt Island, I noticed a shoe box sitting on the counter where one could registered for a free three-day cruise to the Bahama Islands. I had forgotten that I had registered and hadn't told Vera about it, so when she received a call several weeks later from someone telling her we had won the trip, she didn't believe them. She did however, take their phone number. When she told me of the call and I finally remembered having registered, I called them back. That was a nice surprise and a much needed vacation for the two of us.

Vera and I drove to Miami and checked in with the ship terminal. Since we had a few hours until boarding time, I contacted my old friend Bobby Burkett. By then he had been promoted twice and was a sergeant with the major crime task force stationed in Miami.

We had a nice visit with him, and before we left Bobby suggested that I should transfer to Miami, where I could go to work for him and would move up faster in the ranks if I did. I turned down the position he was offering because I didn't want to raise my family in Miami. Later I recalled that during the days I spent with him in training back in Tallahassee, he once told me, "Don't ever turn down anything the highway patrol offers you."

In the fall of 1971 I was issued a new patrol car. When I picked it up in Gainesville, it was a 1972 Dodge Polaris with a 440-cubic-inch engine. Naturally on the way back to Cocoa I had to try it out to see what it would do. All I'll say about it is that it was really fast! I had put about sixteen thousand miles on it when I had a crowd-pleasing accident.

We worked nine-hour shifts with an hour off for dinner. I had just sat down to eat when I received a call to respond to a car on fire with possible occupants trapped inside. I left my dinner on the table and drove up Fiske Boulevard to State Road 520 and turned west. I knew that whatever the problem was, I would be too late to do anything, but I was still hurrying to get to the fire. I was operating my emergency equipment and was going a lot faster than the speed limit.

As I approached the intersection, I noted a car had entered the left turn lane at Clear Lake Road. I continued, still keeping an eye on the car in the turn lane. I did slow some for the intersection but not much, as I figured the approaching driver would stop for me. He didn't. I hit the brakes as he turned, and while slowing I turned to the right and hoped to pass in front of the turning vehicle. By now my headlights were lighting up the interior of the other car and I could see the passenger, a woman, with her mouth open. The thought occurred to me that she was screaming really loud. Instead of hitting his brakes, the driver hit the gas, cutting me off from my planned escape route.

At that point I hit the gas and swerved back left, hoping to go behind his car or turn down Clear Lake Road to the left. I failed to see the unlit utility trailer the car was pulling but managed to get my car sideways. The right side of my car hit the trailer so hard that the impact sheared off the bolts that fastened the trailer hitch to the car frame. The lug bolt pattern from the trailer wheel was embedded in the right-side quarter panel of my car. I was still fighting to straighten out the skidding car when I impacted with the concrete traffic signal pole sitting at the end of the traffic island. After the collision with the post, my car spun around and skidded backward thirty-eight feet.

Finally it stopped and there I was sitting in my car, which was torn up around me and appeared at the time to have no injuries. I was still sitting when the driver of the second car ran over to see if I was hurt. I told him that being around my car or me was not a good idea right then and to please leave. I never saw him again. A little later I did exit my car and found that my ankle hurt pretty badly and figured correctly that it was broken. I was standing, leaning on my car, when a man came running up saying he had heard a state trooper had been killed and wanted to look inside the car. I grabbed him by the shirt and said I was the dead trooper and not so politely asked him to leave. By then the West Cocoa fire chief was on the scene, and seeing the confrontation, he quickly placed me in his car and took me to Wuesthoff Hospital in Rockledge. I have no idea what happened with the car that was on fire.

In the summer of 1972 I had planned to go to my ten-year class reunion back in Kansas, but I found out that the riot squad was scheduled to go to Tallahassee to a SEA-DOCK school on the Florida State University campus. It was a week-long school to help prepare us for any disturbances that might occur at the conventions that were to take place that summer. The school consisted of the army using their people disguised as hippies, black militants, and redneck businessmen. They did everything they could to rile us to the point of over reacting, which they did numerous times. We also learned about civil disobedience laws and how to deal with mass arrests. We were given a book on intelligence already gathered from various sources.

Vera picked me up on Friday and we drove to Kansas. We were there four days of a two-week vacation when I received a call from the Melbourne station advising that I had a ticket waiting for me in Tulsa to fly to Orlando. I managed to stay for one day of the reunion and had to beg out of the other three days. Vera drove me to the Tulsa airport, and I flew to Orlando where I was met by a squad member from Cocoa. He took me by our house and I grabbed my bags and equipment with plans to be in Miami for three to four weeks. We left as soon as I was packed and joined the rest of the team already in Miami.

The weeks before the conventions were filled with meetings and more training. One day we were taken to the Miami Beach convention center for a tour. We met Walter Cronkite and all his news cohosts that we saw on the CBS news every night. We met politicians and their aides and other dignitaries. One hundred and thirty state troopers in uniform in one place attracted a lot of attention.

The FHP unit took on the Miami police department unit in a practice drill at an unused airport hangar. We were the good guys and they were the bad guys, and we whipped them soundly. Then we took on the Dade County Sheriff unit and did it again. We had been in Miami three weeks and we were ready for whatever problems might arise. The first one we faced was the Republican convention.

We lived out by the airport but staged on Miami Beach in a Catholic school. The FHP unit was divided into two units: one was at the convention center and the other was a mobile unit. I was in the mobile unit and we were assigned four men to a car. There were fifteen FHP patrol cars with two or three county sheriff motorcycle escorts. We were called in when the other units were being overwhelmed or for unprotected locations.

The first evening of the convention we were sent to one of the big hotels out on the beach where John Rockefeller was staying and hosting a group. We were there not only to protect the hotel property but as part of the Rockefeller security detail while he was at the hotel. The hotel staged us in a conference room and one squad was stationed outside. Nothing happened that evening. We were pretty far north on Miami Beach, so I don't think anyone knew where Mr. Rockefeller was staying.

Another evening we were called to the convention center when rioters broke down a chainlink fence and were trying to storm the center to disrupt the convention. The rioters were about to overrun our troopers who were assigned to protect the perimeter. They called the mobile squad for assistance.

Our unit formed about a block away from the center and marched in on a back street. The idea was to go in on the rioters from the rear. The order came down to attack, so we started running. Each member was issued a bag of baseball sized teargas grenades that was strapped to his waist. As we were running, someone had not strapped his waist pouch on tightly enough and the grenades banging together caused some of them to explode. The front of the unit started gassing themselves. Those of us in the rear quickly donned our gas masks and sprayed antidote on those that were gassed and helped them with their masks. We also gassed the rioters along with the residents of the street, who were foolishly sitting on their porches watching the goings-on.

The funny thing was that the newspapers were writing bad things about the police and the way we were treating rioters. But during a riot like we were in, behind the convention center, the reporters would stay behind the police lines for protection. During the push I noticed a newspaper photographer behind a parked car where an unknown trooper was taking his cameras away from him and breaking them with his riot baton. No one ever found out who that trooper was, as we all dressed alike and were wearing gas masks. The FHP officials also had us remove our name tags and replace them with ID tags with numbers.

Another night of the convention, the Troop D squad was singled out to block the Lincoln Road Mall near South Beach. We had received intelligence that rioters were going to trash the mall as a distraction for another try at the convention center. Seventeen of us, plus two supervisors, were all there was to protect the Lincoln Road Mall. We were at the north end of the mall when about five thousand people (my estimate) showed up pulling some sort of wagon and playing music and tambourines. I could see we were about to get our butts kicked, when around the corner about a block away came a Cuban demonstration. Now the city fathers went to a lot of trouble to keep the demonstrating groups separated, but, man, we were glad they had messed up this time! The Cubans saw the hippies and were drawn in like a magnet. With that many people fighting and running every which way, our supervisors told us to maintain our positions.

One night at our staging area we received word that the demonstrators were moving down a side road, trashing every business as they went. Colonel Eldridge Beach, our director, had arrived at the command post and wanted to go along with the troopers who were being dispatched. I was carrying a utility vest loaded with teargas canisters, baseball grenades, and thirty-seven-millimeter shells—about seventy-five pounds in all. Colonel Beach, an ex-football player, immediately went to the front and called me forward so he could have the teargas grenades. He started to run about fifty to one hundred feet out in front of all the other troopers, and I struggled to keep up with him. Finally one of the other supervisors came forward and had to get him to wait on the rest of his troopers. We ended up chasing the demonstrators all the way to Collins Avenue and arrested those we could catch.

Another interesting thing was that the military was supplying both the police and the demonstrators with communication devices. I think ours were a little more sophisticated than theirs though. We wore ours inside our helmets, and it was a disk that strapped to the top of our heads and was for listening only. The supervisors wore the same things but had a wire running down their arm to a push button switch held in the hand. With that they were able to talk to us.

The last night of the convention our entire unit was moved into the Eden Roc Hotel, parking our cars underground and out of sight. We staged in the dining room near the lobby. As the demonstrators moved north on Miami Beach Boulevard, we came out on command and blocked the road. The demonstrators saw the policemen moving, but they could not hear commands, so they didn't know what we were about to do. We scared several demonstrators into running. I recall standing in the road with demonstrators about five feet in front of our line. One demonstrator was a young woman about my age. She was screaming at me that we just didn't understand their generation. I handed my baton to the man next to me, removed my helmet so she could see my face, and calmly said to her that I was part of her generation. She was gone by the time I put my helmet back on. I guessed she went looking for someone older to yell at.

The demonstrators sat in the street, blocking Miami Beach Boulevard all the way from our police line to the causeway. We were ordered to arrest anyone that refused to move. We knew we were faced with possibly an uncountable number of arrests that night, but the government had again stepped in. They had rented the Orange Bowl and had chainlink fencing placed all the way around it, and then rented all the rental trucks in Miami, I supposed, for they were lined up for miles. The arrest cards we were to use had large arrest numbers printed on the back. We were to place this number in front of the violator and have our picture made standing with them. We were then to place them in the rental truck to be taken to the Orange Bowl to await a hearing or post bond. Everything worked fine except the part where we had to use two troopers to get the protestors in the trucks, because they had been trained to sit down and go limp. We arrested about 3,600 people that night in August.

By the end of the convention, we were ready to get things over with since we had been working toward this duty for six to eight months. I was glad to get out of Miami for a while. We had to do it all over again for the Democratic convention a month later, but that one wasn't as bad. There just weren't as many protesters or demonstrations as at the previous convention. In all, we were either in school or in Miami for three months.

Back in Cocoa it was difficult to readjust to the routine of a regular shift. Vera and the boys had returned from Kansas. But soon enough things kind of got back to normal for a while.

One day I was on patrol out on I-95. I noticed a car had stopped on the shoulder and the family was standing outside the car. After stopping I figured out that they had just fixed a flat. They had seen a snake out in front of the car and were afraid to get back in. Not knowing what else to do, I decided to shoot the snake.

One of the little ones started to walk toward the snake when I did, but his mother grabbed him and said to him, "You stay back here with us. That man got a gun and that bullet gonna rickajump up and kill you dead." I was laughing so hard that I helped them get in the car and never did kill the snake.

I was called one afternoon to investigate an accident involving a Cocoa City police car near downtown Cocoa. When I arrived there were about fifty to one hundred black demonstrators yelling at the city police who were on the scene. Looking at the demonstrators I saw one person that was louder than all the rest. I called him aside and asked him if he would do me a favor. With an attitude, he asked what I wanted from him. I told him I needed his help clearing the road so I could investigate the accident and get the cars out of there before someone got hurt. I told him I wanted to deputize him so he could move people onto the curb.

I had the man raise his hand and I said to him, "Do you swear to uphold all the laws that are laws in the state of Florida? Say, 'I do'."

He said, "I do." And while he moved his friends out of the street, I cleared the wreck. Later one of the city policemen told me that I had forgotten to un-deputize him. We all had a good laugh over that incident because I had no authority to deputize anyone in the first place.

I was called to the Cocoa Police station late one night. They wouldn't tell me what was going on other than an accident report had to be written up. When I got to the CPD office I met an elderly man who first asked me if I would remove a dead snake from his car hood. Finding his car was easy, since there was a very large snake on the hood along with several bullet holes.

That's when he told me his story: He had been going home on Pluckebaum Road when, "That snake jumped onto the hood of my car and was thrashing around trying to get inside. I stopped, clum over into the backseat, out through the back window, and onto the roof of the car. I had my .25 in my pocket so I shot at that snake until I hit it, and I need a police report." By then I was laughing so hard it took several minutes before I could proceed with the incident report.

I kept the dead snake in a box to show since it was a rather large rattlesnake. There were not many people to show it to on the midnight shift, so before the gas station I used for service opened, I took the dead snake and coiled it up in their front door. I left it there, and later when I went to get my car serviced, it was still lying there and the guys were using one of the service bay doors to get in and out. I got another laugh from that after I told them it was dead.

I pulled another practical joke at the Sinclair gas station at State Road 520 and Plumosa one midnight shift. The operator had a habit of catching me away from my car when I would stop for fuel, and he would lock and close the doors. I hadn't made myself a spare key yet at that time, so I always had to get a coat hanger and unlock the car. After he did that a few more times, I decided that given an opportunity, I would get even.

One night on the midnight shift I saw that he was working. I waited until about daylight and saw he was nodding off in the office. Now the station had a long hose wrapped all the way around it, so if anyone drove over it, a bell would sound in the station and alert the operator that a customer had entered the lot. I took the hose and unwound it from the station and dragged it out into the highway. Then I went across the street to watch. A few cars drove over the hose, waking up the operator. He would look around, and not seeing anyone, he would get comfortable and go back to nodding. When rush hour started, the bell went nuts and had the poor guy running every which way. He finally cut the line since he couldn't get it all out of the highway.

There was another accident that I worked on Pluckebaum Road that was outside the norm for accidents. A family piled into their car out west of the accident site and was headed to town. There were too many people in the car, most of whom were children. Pluckebaum Road was an east–west road that, although dirt, was a convenient route to town if a driver wanted to stay off State Road 520, a busy four-lane highway.

As the driver headed east, he was momentarily distracted, undoubtedly from the environment inside the crowded car. The car ran off the road, which had no shoulders, and turned upside down in a drainage canal. The driver managed to escape and said that he reached inside the car and pulled out two of the children. When I arrived, the old man was so confused that he could not tell me how many people were still in the car. All he could think to tell me was that he had lost his wallet, which had twenty-five dollars in it. We knew we had fatalities but not how many until divers from the fire department started pulling bodies out. Seven fatalities were pulled from the overturned car.

Seven fatalities is a lot for a single car wreck, and of course as word spread, we ended up with a mess as the press and neighbors started trying to get to the scene. The sheriff department and the FHP closed the road, which caused tempers to rise. I had worked several accidents with multiple fatalities, but this was the most I ever worked in one wreck.

Another odd wreck occurred outside the south gate of Cape Kennedy on Courtenay Parkway. The traffic coming out the gate had slowed almost to a stop for a turning vehicle. This portion of Courtenay Parkway was a two-lane highway and traffic tie-ups were not uncommon. A woman driver started to slow but then she must have hit the gas rather than the brake because she could not get the car to stop. It kept going faster and faster and collided with the right rear of the car directly in front of hers. She then went onto the shoulder, still accelerating, and as she tried to get back onto the pavement, her car collided with two more stopped cars. One of those was pushed into a fourth car. Her car finally slowed but managed to hit another car going in the opposite direction before coming to a stop. There were many cars involved and she was hysterical.

I had the driver sit in my car as I completed the paperwork, and I offered to either call someone for her or take her home. She opted for me to take her home. She was almost calmed down by the time we got there. As she exited my car and shut the door, the passenger side window shattered. It could have been the heat, stress from the angle I was sitting, or anything, I guess, but when the window shattered it sent the lady back into hysterics. Her family was home, thank goodness, and I got some help for her and finally was able to leave.

I worked an accident involving a pedestrian near North Banana River Drive on State Road 520 one night when I was working the midnight shift. An intoxicated sailor was standing near a local hangout named the Cork Lounge, trying to hitch a ride. He was so intoxicated that he was hitching in the westbound lanes and he actually needed to go east. He was standing in the middle of the right lane rather than on the shoulder.

Being an unlit area, after several near misses he was struck by a westbound car. When I arrived, I could tell he had a couple of broken legs at least. Checking his ID, I found out he was a British sailor off a submarine docked at the Cape Canaveral turn basin. With no other way to contact them, I went out there and met the commanding officer and told him about his injured sailor.

I had wanted to be a submariner when I had first joined the navy in 1963, but they needed hospital corpsmen more so I became a corpsman. When I told the submarine captain that bit of information, he invited me to come back out the next day for a tour of their sub. The British really knew how to treat a policeman, or at least one that was aiding one of their comrades. It ended up they had to leave their buddy behind to get well, and he flew back to England where, I presume, he rejoined the submarine after his broken legs healed.

Where the causeways cross the rivers, the roads are built on landfills. To keep the river flowing, relief bridges are built at intervals before and after the main high-rise bridge. The relief bridges are smaller and low to the road and are not built for boat traffic, unless they are small boats. The high-rise bridge is built across the main channel. People in Brevard County hang lanterns off the relief bridges that attract shrimp. The shrimp can be dipped out of the river with specially made dip nets. They are usually attached to long extension handles that can reach the water from the bridges.

One night I was in the process of trying to overtake a violator. As I was accelerating, I saw white tennis shoes crossing the highway in my path. That's all I saw since the area was unlit and the pedestrian was wearing dark clothes. I never did see the long pole and net he was carrying as he was changing sides of the road. I hit the pole, which, thank goodness, was in his off-side hand. Rather than cause him injury, I just knocked the pole out of his hand. I called out my supervisor and we worked up the accident; I had another accident credited to me. Although this one and the big one I had when I had a car turn in front of me, were not my fault, they were still my accidents.

Another time I was called out to I-95 to deal with cows on the highway that were causing motorists to swerve. I headed out there and found a couple of big yearling calves loose on the northbound shoulder. I called Charlie Ragsdale for some help, and after locating the hole in the fence, I started trying to herd the cows back toward it. The idea was to block their progress and herd them to a point where they would find the hole and go back through.

Somewhere along the way one of the cows got mad and came after me since I was on foot. Off I went in a foot race, headed toward the safety of my car. I leaped onto the hood of my car, denting it in the process. My shoes were damp from the grass, and I slid across the top and kept from sliding off the back by grabbing the blue light as I passed it. Meanwhile Charlie had showed up and parked directly behind me. The calf circled my car, butting it wherever there was a light. Finally it turned and butted and broke the grill on Charlie's car.

We finally got the owner of the cows to the scene. He roped and hog-tied the calf and dragged it into a Volkswagen minivan. However, he failed to tie it up enough, and after closing the doors to the van, the cow got loose and tore up the inside of his vehicle. I had about one thousand dollars' worth of damage and Charlie received about five hundred dollars' worth to his car. When I leaped to the hood of my car, I seemed to have ripped the rear out of the seat of my pants also. Somehow my old friend Wayne, the newspaper reporter, had heard about the incident over his scanner and was on the scene. There were no pictures in the paper this time, though he had an artist draw a cartoon for the article. It showed a trooper standing on the roof of his patrol car, shaking a fist at the cow while his other hand held the seat of his britches.

During this phase of bad luck, I was working traffic out on I-95 one evening. I clocked a northbound speeding vehicle, and I started to turn around. As I crossed the median, the rear window of my patrol car blew from the twist I put on the car when I turned through the ditch. It was a borrowed car—such was the way my luck had been running.

One midnight shift I responded to an accident where a semi, loaded with fresh vegetables out of the Everglades, had turned over on I-95. When I arrived, one of the northbound lanes was blocked by the overturned truck and its spilled load. Before being taken to the hospital, the driver asked me to call his boss and told me to take some of the vegetables for myself.

I called the on-call supervisor and advised that I would probably be at this accident the rest of the night, which he approved. I also called my midnight shift zone partner, E. C. Stewart, and advised him. It wasn't long before E. C. was also on the scene, since there was very little happening that time of night. We both loaded up our cars with vegetables and left one at a time to deliver them to other troopers. It was hard not to do that since our pay normally would not make it to the end of the month and the state was refusing to let us work off-duty jobs.

When we took the vegetables to a trooper in the middle of the night, we left them on the porch for them to find when they woke up. E. C. and I stayed out there the rest of the night, and when morning came, so did a crew from the insurance company. They had found a local vegetable market to purchase the undamaged portion of the load, which was 90 percent of it. As they were cleaning up the mess, the new owner came up to me and said I could fill my car up with whatever I could get in it. E. C. and I filled our cars again and left. What a haul! Maybe it was not totally the right thing to do, but they were giving it to us and we certainly could use it.

I generally was able to avoid altercations with violators by keeping a level head and not allowing anyone to push me too far—but not always. One evening I was checking traffic with VASCAR on State Road 520. I clocked a speeder through the zone and started to go after the speeding car. The driver must have realized he was being pursued, as he began trying to elude me.

I chased the violator off State Route 520 onto A Lane. This was a neighborhood where a few years earlier a mob had taken the gun away from a deputy, who was attempting to serve a warrant, and shot him in the hand with his own gun. I had this in mind when I finally got the speeder to stop.

From the start I knew the situation was trouble. The speeder had a woman in the car and started arguing as soon as I asked for his driver's license. I returned to my car and checked the driver's name for warrants. I also declared an emergency and asked for immediate backup, having noticed that a crowd was forming.

On returning to the violator's car, I found that he had exited it. The violator became agitated and refused to sign the citation I had written. I advised him that if he refused, I would have to put him in jail. He still refused, so I started to take him into custody. That was when he took a swing at me. He started grabbing for my gun, and we started scuffling and fighting. Every time I hit him and knocked him to the ground, the crowd, who at this point had done nothing but watch, cheered him back onto his feet. Then we had to do it all over again.

At one point I attempted to strike a sensitive point with my big, five-cell flashlight. Striking someone on the leg in the right place will disable them for a short while if the nerve is hit hard enough. As I swung the flashlight, the batteries came out. There went the flashlight—it was nothing but a shell with the batteries missing.

No help arrived and I was in a real mess! Finally the violator's wife appeared with her brothers and they separated us and dispersed the crowd. She asked me what was going on, and I told her that her husband and his lady friend were speeding and he had refused to sign the citation. That's when she found out about the girlfriend and my part of the fight was over!

By that time another trooper had arrived on the scene. He said he had not been told that this was a declared emergency so had not been in a hurry to get to me. He had actually stopped and written a couple of tickets along the way.

The violator's brothers-in-law held the man while I cuffed him. The violator said he would go to jail with the newly arrived trooper but refused to go with me. When asked why, he replied that he knew this fight was not over and figured I would stop somewhere before I got him to jail and finish it. So he did go to jail but not with me.

At the jail I found out the violator had choked me to the point that I had a bruise already starting on my neck, and my shirt was torn where he had tried to rip off my badge.

Another time I arrested a violator for driving under the influence. I got him in my car without having to use the handcuffs and took him to jail. After placing the violator in the holding tank, I started the booking process. A deputy who was already booking in a prisoner asked who had brought in my prisoner. When I told him I had, he said that last time this man had been arrested it took six deputies to get him to jail. I guess it's just how you talk to people—but then again, everyone doesn't listen.

One evening on Merritt Island I clocked a speeder on Sykes Creek Parkway. When I turned around in pursuit, the violator saw me and started going faster. We reached North Banana River Drive when he realized he was pretty much caught, so he pulled into the Merritt Island East fire station parking lot. When I turned in, he quickly cut a U-turn and started back across Sykes Creek Parkway, headed the other direction. I cut across the curb and came off the parking lot right behind him. As we drove he was watching me in his rear view mirror. I guess he wasn't watching the road, because the next thing I knew, he ran off into the swamp that bordered both sides of the road. The car spun around and overturned onto its right side.

I called for rescue and assistance, and realizing the occupants were not exiting the vehicle, I went into the water and climbed onto the side of the overturned car. I saw that there were three boys inside and all were lying in water and so tangled up that none could get free. I climbed in and helped them untangle and escape drowning. By then help had arrived, so I had the boys wade ashore to be detained. As I was climbing off the car, my muddy hands slipped off the handhold and I grabbed a hot tailpipe. I received first, second, and third degree burns on my right hand from that.

One night I was the only trooper on duty in the county and had stopped at Courtenay Parkway and State Road 520 for fuel. While I was there, I received a call from Richard Warden, the midnight shift dispatcher in Palm Bay. He advised me that someone was beating on the back door of the patrol station. I advised him to not let them in but to send them around to the front lobby.

A short time later Richard came back to the radio and said no one had been at the rear door. He started to say something else and was cut off. My attempts to contact him failed.

I finished fueling up and headed to the Palm Bay station. I contacted the Orlando station, advised them of the situation in Palm Bay and asked them to contact the Palm Bay police department and send someone. In the meantime I hit US Route 1 and headed south, still trying to contact the station. I arrived in record time and found Richard and a city policeman in the station. Richard had a knot on his head from being knocked out, and the unknown intruder had trashed the patrol station.

I contacted the shift supervisor at home and apprised him of the situation. By the end of the night the corporal, sergeant, and the station lieutenant were all at the station. I had to stay at the station for a statement so another trooper was called out to finish my shift. There were no happy troopers in Brevard County that night.

It was never discovered who had entered the station that night and nothing appeared taken, just the building trashed. This incident changed the way stations were operated from then on. Statewide, all stations that were open after midnight had electric door locks installed, and no one could enter unless the dispatcher knew who was at the door. Everyone else had to use an intercom to talk to the dispatcher.

One evening I was working traffic on State Road 520 in east Merritt Island and saw about thirty-five to forty motorcyclist headed toward Cocoa Beach. I decided to stop all of them since the rearmost motorcyclist had a burned-out taillight. I called in, stating I was going 10-50 (stopping violator) on all these motorcycles. We had no remote radios back then, so I didn't know that the dispatcher after a short time had called for reinforcements to head my way. He had been unable to get me back on the radio and, rightly so, thought I was having trouble. Naturally I checked all the motorcycles, since they all stopped for the one. I got a couple of expired tags and an expired driver's license. I released all the riders before any backup arrived. Those that eventually responded were the Cocoa Beach PD, Cocoa PD, Brevard sheriff office, and the one other trooper who was in the central area.

I was working the day shift when I was called to a multi-car accident at State Road 520 and Plumosa Avenue. When I arrived on the scene, I found a truck towing a lowboy trailer sitting on the side of the road. Damaged cars were scattered along the shoulder. The driver of the truck stated that he had finished his job and loaded his tractor onto the trailer. He then tied it down and was headed home. When he stopped for the signal at Plumosa, the tractor jumped off the trailer, started itself, and began hitting cars. It finally came to rest in a storefront where it was stuck against a wall with the tires still digging for traction. The investigation revealed that although the driver had put the tractor on the trailer at the job site, he had allowed it to choke down, killing the engine. He failed to turn off the ignition and used only one chain binder to hold the tractor in place. Due to the slack created by the tractor during transport, it rolled forward enough to start itself. Then it was a matter of crashing into anything that got in the way.

Our district had lots of cookouts and parties. These events built lifelong friendships, not only with the troopers that came but with a lot of other people we invited. We generally invited county commissioners, fire district supervisors, safety people, and select others. Parties were held in county buildings or fire stations. Cookouts were at Russ France's home or sometimes at the Jack Story Ranch out near the St. Johns River. Troopers were the cooks, and we cooked donated chicken, pork, or beef on the smokers. At Russ's we mostly had either fried or smoked fish.

I got to know the volunteer firemen, wrecker drivers, ambulance drivers, and EMT's. We were just a bunch of young men doing what young men do: making a living, raising families, and enjoying being around each other. Working long, odd hours is a hard task for policemen and emergency personnel and it often causes divorces.

My own personal life was in shambles, and Vera and I were trying to work out our problems, but I found that Brevard County was not the place we could do that. In order to save our marriage I agreed to Vera's request and put in for a transfer back home to Pensacola.

After three months I had not received an acknowledgment of my request, so I contacted the district commander and the troop commander, who both checked with general headquarters on my status. There was no record of the letter being received, but fortunately I had sent the letter through the troop office in Orlando. Within two weeks not only did I receive an acknowledgment letter, but I also received a transfer letter. We were going home.

PART III:

Troop A, Escambia County District, Pensacola

August 1974–January 1989

Escambia County is the westernmost county in the panhandle of the State of Florida. The State of Alabama lies across the state line both to the west and the north. All traffic headed east into Florida either traveled on the newly opened I-10 or US Route 90 or US Route 98. That remains the case even today.

Troop A of the Florida Highway Patrol consists of ten counties that stretch from the Alabama State line to the Apalachicola River. The counties are Escambia, Santa Rosa, Okaloosa, Walton, Holmes, Washington, Bay, Jackson, Calhoun, and Gulf. The troop headquarters is located in Panama City, Bay County. Pensacola District is made up of Escambia and Santa Rosa counties, with Pensacola serving as the district office.

The first FHP station in Pensacola was located at the bridge tenders building, which was located in the center of the Pensacola Bay Bridge. This was where any information that was received was dispatched to the troopers. A lot of times, due to the broad width of territories a trooper had to work, a trooper would have to call in several times a day to receive information, such as regarding accidents. The station was moved to the north end of the bay bridge several years later, as the work load became heavier and additional troopers were added. As that building became too small, it was again moved across the road to a triangle area between Gregory Street and Seventeenth Avenue. It was at this location when I transferred to Pensacola. The district commander was Lieutenant Clark C. Waters.

Prior to my arrival, the Escambia county sheriff's department handled all accidents in the county. There was also a problem with wreckers, so the state stepped in and started handling accidents, which required more troopers. The FHP had about eight troopers working in Escambia County when this change took place, so they increased the number from eight to twenty-two in a matter of months. I was one of the first of those additional troopers.

I had been stationed in Pensacola when I was in the navy, but upon my return, I learned that I really did not know the city. As a state trooper I had to learn the roads, the traffic patterns, the people, and where the trouble areas of the county were located, such as the bars and dangerous intersections. But by the time I arrived in Pensacola, I was a seasoned trooper and knew what to look for and usually where to look.

I only rode one day with another trooper to obtain the court procedures and other important information. The rest I was expected to learn as I went. I also spent time talking to the district sergeant and the local corporal, who would be my immediate supervisors. Finally I met Lieutenant Waters. He was someone that I had already heard a lot about; he was one of the legends of the FHP. His very first comment to me was, "Don't ever lie to me, and I mean never, and we'll get along fine. If I feel a lie is necessary, I need to be in on it so we both will know what we are lying about." That pretty much set the tone for my time in Pensacola.

I was used to writing about one hundred citations a month and noted on the charts that most of these troopers were writing maybe fifteen to thirty a month. I commented about that to Lieutenant Waters, who said that he didn't care how many I wrote, but if I wrote that many, I wouldn't have a problem with him. I worked the day shift the remainder of the month, and then I was put on the 3:00 p.m. to 11:00 p.m. shift.

I hadn't been in Pensacola but just a few months when troopers started coming to me and saying I was making them look bad. I said, "You have that backward. You're making me look really good!"

I was staying with my friends Jack and Edith Buffler while I was waiting for Vera and the boys to arrive. She not only had to get the house ready to sell but had to get things boxed up for the movers. Vera left Rockledge with the two boys, a dog, a cat, and house plants, with our canoe on the roof of the car and the camper trailer being towed behind. She did that without any help from me since I was already at work in Pensacola. In the meantime, I had located a rental house for us, and when the movers arrived a few days later with our furniture, several of the local troopers came to help us move in.

While staying with Jack I got involved with an off-duty event that would help me personally later. Just before I closed out my shift one evening at midnight, I had heard that a robbery had occurred at a convenience store in west Pensacola. I went ahead and checked out and left for the night. Jack was still up, so we sat outside talking. Suddenly I heard a motorcycle a couple streets over. The description of the getaway vehicle in the robbery was a motorcycle with no muffler and two occupants. Jack told me that there were a couple of youths that had such a motorcycle that lived over in the area where we had heard the noisy motorcycle. He told me where they lived, and I returned to my car and called in about the motorcycle and that I was en route to check it out.

I went to the area where I knew the house was located and saw the youths putting the motorcycle in the woods and covering it with weeds. When I pulled in to talk to them, they ran. I caught one and he had the bag with cash in it. I talked to his family that was home and found that the second boy lived a few houses down the road. By this time assistance was there and I turned the investigation over to the county sheriff department. As a result of this off duty capture and arrest, I was selected later in the year as the state trooper of the year by the local Friends of Law Enforcement.

One evening shift I was called to an accident where a car had struck a cow that had escaped its pasture. When I arrived, the cow was in the ditch, struggling with multiple broken legs. I asked around to see if anyone knew the owner, but I got no response from the small crowd that had gathered.

I continued working the accident but noticed a small knot of men standing off to one side. I approached them and asked if they knew the owner of the cow. The oldest man asked what would happen to the owner if he came forward. I quoted him the stock law, and he admitted that it was his cow. He said he had just purchased several and they were not yet accustomed to the pasture they were put in. This one had broken down the fence and gotten out. I asked what he wanted to do with the cow since it would have to be put down. He asked if I could do that for him and said he would remove the beef himself. I shot the cow for the man, and some of his boys started loading it for removal.

We tracked the cow back to the man's property and found where it had broken the fence down and gotten loose. While we were tracking the cow, I casually asked if they knew someone out here in the area who might have property for sale. Returning to the scene, I finished my investigation and was wrapping things up when the owner, Walter Jones, came up to me and said that he wanted me to stop by his house when my shift was over.

I went to the man's house later and found the whole family outside, watching the boys skin and butcher the cow. Walter wanted me to have a choice roast from the cow, which I refused. As we stood around talking, he said that he wanted me to go out to his house the next day, as he had something to show me. I bid them good evening, and when I returned to my car, I found a large rump roast wrapped in butcher paper sitting in the floor of the car.

The next morning I took Vera and returned to the Jones house once more to meet Walter and see what he had on his mind. He showed us a couple acres that he had for sale and offered to sell them to us. We agreed to the price he quoted and shook hands.

As we left Mrs. Jones handed us enough frozen vegetables from her freezer to fill a large grocery sack. That day was the beginning of a friendship that lasted until they both died. Just before Mrs. Jones died, she instructed her daughter, who was managing their affairs, that she should sell their remaining property to me. The total was another two and a half acres. That included where their family home had stood and a wood lot.

In the fall my friend Charlie Ragsdale transferred from Cocoa to Pensacola. Once I went back there, I guess he wanted to do the same. Charlie arrived about three months after I did.

We both had friends in Cocoa, so we made plans for a hunting trip to the Smith Creek area of the Apalachicola National Wildlife area south of Tallahassee. Charlie and I met four of our Cocoa friends at Smith Creek and had five days of good hunting. Over that period I think we got a deer, a wild hog, and dozens of squirrels.

The camp was located on a bluff overlooking a swamp near the Ochlockonee River. The last night there, as we were sitting around the campfire going over old times and the hunt, I thought I heard someone yelling. No one else heard the yells, so I stepped away from the camp and returned the call. I thought the person said he was lost but wasn't sure. I went back and told the others that I was going out in the swamp to see if I could locate this person.

I took my lantern and strung it up in a tall pine tree so it could be seen a long way off. Charlie said he would go with me, and we struck out across the swamp. We went out to a point where we could just still see the lantern, and I then left Charlie and headed in the direction I had last heard the man.

Soon I came to the river and yelled again. I was about a quarter mile away from the man who had started yelling continuously. When I finally reached where he was, I found him on the other side of the river. He said he had become separated from his hunting party and had been lost all day. He needed help getting back to his camp but had no idea where the camp was.

The man wanted me to swim the river and help him get back. After a quick assessment, I figured if I drowned swimming the river, then he would probably die also due to exposure. So I told him that if I were to help him, he was the one who had to swim the river. I proceeded to explain my reasoning and what he needed to do. I wanted him to come to me and suggested he find a dry log, take off his boots, and using the laces, tie the boots and his rifle to the log and push it in front of him to cross the river. I was going to come in if he ran into trouble. The log worked and he made it safely across the Ochlockonee River.

As the man rested, he gave me his name and said he was a legislative aid and thought he could locate where the rest of his party was camped if he could get to the highway. So after resting we started back across the swamp and finally saw Charlie's light. It was then a matter of following the light from the lantern on the ridge to get back to our camp. Once we reached the camp, we again rested and the other men plied our new-found friend with coffee and a little "snake bite medicine".

I returned the lost man safely to his camp and to his friends. They had looked all day for him and never came close to his location. When I told them where I found him, they realized he was miles away in the wrong direction from where they had been hunting. I left my name and Charlie's name with our new friend and returned to camp. We finished our camp, said our good-byes, and then headed home.

Several weeks later I received a copy of a letter this person had written to the department, commending me on saving him. Sadly, he only listed Charlie as Trooper Charlie, so Charlie did not get a copy of the letter nor was he recognized as being part of the rescue. This unfortunate deletion cost me a good friend. Charlie eventually returned to Brevard County and remained there until he retired.

I was called one evening to assist a trooper in the next county over, Santa Rosa County. He had been in pursuit of someone wanted by the Escambia county sheriff's department for felony warrants. Trooper Steve Bates chased him and exchanged gunfire with the car occupant. Bates finally trapped the car as the driver attempted a U-turn. Since he would be required to remain on the scene to assist in completing the investigation, he requested that I meet him and take his prisoner to the Escambia County jail.

I met Steve where he asked me and loaded the prisoner to transport him to jail. He said that the violator had tried to escape from his car while he was driving to meet me.

Steve reminded me to be careful since I would be alone with this guy. I had no idea how to get to the jail from that location, so of course I took a wrong turn and was actually headed toward the interstate.

Just before the interstate I was stopped behind a fuel tanker truck at a red light. We did not have prisoner cages in our cars, so I had handcuffed the prisoner with his hands behind him and seat belted him in the right front seat. While stopped, the prisoner started struggling with the lap belt and managed to get it off. Being double-jointed, he was able to slip his hands from behind his back, get them under his legs, and put out in front of him. He did that while all the time I was struggling with him to keep him fastened in. He and I went out the passenger door onto the road, fighting, him trying to get my gun and me trying to subdue him.

We managed to roll under the tanker and were under it when I heard the driver trying to shift gears to start. Obviously the light had changed to green and he had not seen us. The tanker rolled far enough forward where he could see my car with the bar light lit up. He immediately stopped, without rolling over us, and came back to see what I wanted. That's when he saw us fighting under his truck. The tanker driver joined the ruckus and managed to sit on the prisoner's legs. That allowed me to get a second set of handcuffs on the prisoner and get his arms behind him and lock them down.

Meanwhile, Trooper Bates had been trying to call me on the radio, and of course I couldn't answer, so everyone was looking for me. They found us as we were, under the truck, with the driver sitting on the prisoner and me holding the rest of him down. I had a hard time getting Bates to stop laughing long enough to get the prisoner back in the car and onto jail.

Back in the 1970s, we still had low-band radios, the kind with the whip antenna like you saw on the police cars in the old TV shows. These radios did not have a long range. On the peninsula of Florida one busy station could completely overpower and block the radio usage of another station to the point where some troopers could not communicate with it. In some areas messages would have to be relayed because of distances between the car and the station. There was also a phenomenon that happened when a heavy cloud cover existed. The radio signals would skip on the clouds and could be heard many miles from the point of origin.

This skip happened to me one afternoon as I was called to an accident. A house mover was pulling a house along a state road when the driver swerved to miss a traffic signal and hit a stopped car on the side of the road. Always up for a wisecrack, when I arrived and saw what had occurred, I contacted the dispatcher and said, "You're not going to believe this, but a house actually hit a car." The skip took the radio signal four hundred miles down to Brevard County, from where I had just been transferred, and of course the shift troopers heard my transmission. One of my friends down there replied, "It could only happen to Black Cloud." The irony of it was funny, but it also let the Pensacola troopers know that I was the Black Cloud that everyone had heard about.

Because of the amount of activity I was producing (arrests, warnings, and faulty equipment cards), I started getting selected for details that normally went to troopers that had been in the district longer than I had. One of the first details was a state funeral in Daytona. A state senator from that area had died, and the FHP was providing a twenty-four-hour honor guard until his funeral. We were selected from all over the state for this task. The troopers who worked that detail were divided into groups of two, and we worked the honor guard detail two hours on and four hours off for two or three days. It was an honor to be selected for these types of details.

In the spring of 1975, I was assigned to I-10, from the Alabama/Florida state line thirty-two miles east to the Santa Rosa/Okaloosa County line. My job on I-10 was not only to enforce traffic laws but to make regular scheduled circuits of that area to assist motorists who might be experiencing car trouble.

I received such a call that a motorist was broken down on the Escambia Bay I-10 bridge. This bridge consisted of two separate bridges, each with two lanes: one bridge for eastbound traffic and the other for westbound traffic. The bridges were three miles long with no emergency lane, and the center span rose sixty-five to eighty-five feet to allow barge traffic to pass under. The center of this raised section also marked the boundary between Escambia and Santa Rosa counties.

I headed out to check the bridge, but before I could get there, Trooper Joe Davis arrived on scene and relayed to me that I was needed out there to assist with slowing traffic. As I passed the stalled car that was sitting on the westbound bridge, I could see from the opposite bridge that it was stopped just over the hump on the downhill side of the rise. I went to the end of the eastbound bridge and turned around and stopped about three-fourths of the way up the uphill side of the westbound bridge, just inside the Santa Rosa County line. I stopped about 250 feet behind Trooper Davis, who had his emergency light on. He was stopped just behind the disabled vehicle.

I immediately turned on every emergency light I had and exited the vehicle. I also took a red flag, and as an extra precaution, I moved away from my car. I had been directing traffic for about ten minutes when I noticed that an approaching car in the right lane was neither slowing nor attempting to change lanes. When I realized that a crash was imminent, I started running.

Trooper Davis, who saw the car crash into my car, started yelling, "Run faster!" When I looked back, my car was gaining on me! I first thought of jumping off the bridge but realized that it was too high up, so I ran faster. Finally, as I passed Joe, he yelled at me that I could stop. I continued to Joe's car and radioed that I had been involved in an accident and needed a supervisor. Joe went down and checked on the injured as I called for an ambulance. I approached the other car and saw that an elderly lady was the driver. I talked to her until the ambulance arrived and she kept saying to me, "How did you get here so quick?" I told her several times that I was here first and she had run into my car.

Several years later I became a member of Beulah Baptist Church. While there I met a member who found out that I was a state trooper. He said that his mother had run into a state trooper several years earlier and that I might possibly know her. After learning where the accident happened, I told him that she had run into me. He then told me that she ran our local polling precinct. The next time we voted I took the photographs of the accident and showed them to her. I told her that when she hit my patrol car, she hit it so hard that she literally "knocked it into the next county." That's exactly what had happened; it was shoved from Santa Rosa County to Escambia County, a distance of just over one hundred feet.

The woman told me that her husband was a preacher and they had visited a church in DeFuniak Springs, Florida, and were on their way home. The weather was cool and the sun had been shining in their faces all the way home, and she said that she had dozed off and had no idea what she had hit.

I found out that in Troop A they still had what was known as "midnight riders." These were supervisors that came out unannounced, often from another district, checking on the midnight troopers. There was no regularly scheduled supervisor out on the midnight shifts.

One night there were two of us working the two-county area that consisted of Escambia and Santa Rosa counties. Another trooper and I were sitting in the median on I-10, watching traffic and visiting, when we received a coded message from the dispatcher alerting us that the midnight rider had checked in by phone. We pulled into a stand of trees not far from where we were sitting and waited.

Sure enough, it wasn't long before Corporal J. D. Judson drove by. We were the only troopers who were supposed to be out that time of night. To let Corporal

Judson know we had spotted him, I called out over the radio for the trooper traveling west on I-10 to identify himself to me.

After receiving no response, I said, "Who goes there with his nose in the air?" I still never received a response, but about thirty minutes later we were notified that he had gone home.

On May 8, 1978, a loaded passenger plane, a Boeing 727, landed short of the runway and ended up in the Escambia Bay. I was working the 3:00 p.m. to 11:00 p.m. shift when that happened. Several troopers responded, and with the assistance of a passing barge, all the passengers but three were rescued from the water. I was just getting off shift, so I quickly returned to work and went to the station to assist with the phone lines.

Another incident later involved a derailed freight train along Scenic Highway in Pensacola. The train had derailed near some homes overlooking the bay, and one car loaded with anhydrous ammonia ruptured. Several fatalities occurred in that incident, and again I went to the station to assist the dispatchers with the phone lines. An area one half mile inland from the tracks and one mile long was evacuated, and of course all police departments were overwhelmed with the evacuation and phone calls.

I always enjoyed finding an area where I could find activity. I found one such area when I was working US Route 29 for a couple of hours and then switching over to State Road 297. I found that as word got around that I was working traffic on US Route 29, drivers would cut over to the parallel road to avoid me. When I stopped one speeding vehicle that was pulling a stock trailer on State Road 297, the driver said, "Why aren't you over on US Route 29 where you're supposed to be?'

One afternoon I was called to an accident on Highway 29 in the McDavid Community. When I arrived I saw a pulpwood truck crashed against a tree where Roach Road intersected with US Route 29. There was one person still in the vehicle. He was conscious and told me he was not the driver. I asked if he remembered what had happened, and he told me the story.

He and his two buddies had left the woods with a load of pulpwood. The old truck had bad brakes, and he had told the driver that he was afraid of the truck. Assured that everything was all right, he slid into the middle seat while one friend sat by the right door and the driver climbed in the other side. Off they went, headed to the St. Regis Paper Mill in Cantonment with their load of wood.

On the downhill section of Roach Road, the driver attempted to slow down as they approached US Route 29. The brakes on the old truck decided that was the time to quit and failed on the hill. The out-of-control truck was gaining speed as it went down the hill, and the driver decided it was time to bail out, so he exited the truck. The passenger on the right, seeing the driver bail out, decided that was the time for him to get out also, so he too bailed out. This left the passenger sitting in the center. He was straddling the shifter lever in the floor and was unable to follow his friends. His exact words were, "One foo jumped out one side and the other foo jumped out the other side and them foos boff lef me in da truck." He also informed me that he was getting new friends.

Gil Wilson, a weight trooper from central Florida who had a portable scale trailer, was scheduled to be in our area for one day to work the area around the paper mill in Cantonment. I met him and a local weight trooper, Jack Goodwin, in Cantonment, and they set up and started weighing trucks. I noticed in the first few minutes that I was seeing trucks with no tags, expired inspection stickers, and lots of broken lights. I was assigned to direct traffic, so I was unable to stop and write tickets for all those violations. I got on the radio and called for several auxiliary troopers to come and assist.

On their arrival I had some of them directing traffic while others were checking faulty equipment, tags, inspection stickers, and driver's licenses. I started writing citations, and soon thereafter, Gill and Jack came over with their ticket books and wanted some of the activity I was generating. At the end of the day I had over one hundred faulty equipment cards. These were cards that notified the driver that they had lights broken or burned out and needed to make repairs or face a citation. I wrote ninety citations in three different ticket books in a six-hour shift. That was the most citations I had ever written on one shift.

One afternoon, several of us troopers were discussing the upcoming boxing match between Muhammad Ali and George Foreman. It was scheduled to be on television that evening. We decided that if we were not busy, we should go somewhere safe and try to watch it.

I suggested that since we had recently built a house in the country, we could go there and there would be plenty of room. Word quickly spread to the entire shift what we were going to do. I knew Vera and the boys would be at a school function that evening, so I thought we would be fine and no one would know what we were doing. Late into the shift, I headed home, dragged out the extension cord and the TV, and set the TV up in the driveway. That way we could listen to any calls we might get and see the fight. Some troopers had arrived and still others were on their way.

In the meantime, unknown to us, Vera and the boys were headed home. She said that as she turned onto the highway leading toward home, she saw a highway patrol car in front of her going in the same direction she was headed. She then noticed a second one behind her, which also turned the same direction she was headed. As she turned onto our street, both patrol cars also turned. Vera also knew that if I had been injured or killed, the family would be notified in person.

Afraid that bad news awaited her, she was reluctant to enter our yard. The boys convinced her that they had to go in and find out what had happened. As she entered the backyard, she saw all the troopers and the TV, with all of us standing around watching the fight. She never said anything to the other troopers, but she unloaded on me.

Suddenly all my friends flushed like a covey of quail and abandoned me to my fate. It was not a pretty sight. Needless to say, we never saw the rest of the fight. It was very thoughtless of me to not let her know what we were doing. Thirty-three years later, we still laugh about that. But at the time it was very serious business.

Early one afternoon I was working traffic on I-10 west of Pensacola when I noticed a vehicle with a woman and a small child sitting in the median with a flat. I stopped and started assisting. Another trooper, Buddy Charles, arrived to assist with traffic if needed. We all made note of some afternoon thunder clouds to our west and estimated they were far enough away that we would be able to finish changing the tire before the rain reached us.

We were about halfway finished when there was a clap of thunder and a flash. Lightning had hit a pine tree just across the highway, probably less than one hundred feet from where we were standing. The concussion blew both our hats off and made our hair stand on end. It also blew the hubcaps off my car. We immediately ceased changing the tire, and I put the lady and her child in my car, where we stayed until the threat of the storm passed.

Most of the troopers in the Pensacola district were senior troopers, as this was an area that it took seniority to get transferred into. That changed when the FHP decided we needed a female trooper in Troop A. The female was assigned to the Pensacola district. Sandy was a tall woman, nearly as tall as my six feet. The district commander had her ride with several troopers during the course of her training, but I was assigned as her field training officer when she started learning what it would take to become a state trooper. Not only did she become a very good trooper, but we became friends and remained so even after I retired and took a job in the private sector.

Sandy was the first of several young troopers that I was field training officer to in Escambia. It was always a pleasure for me to train these new troopers, and I hope I instilled in them the work ethic that my field training officer taught me.

Around this same time I was asked to become an assistant instructor for the Florida Highway Patrol Auxiliary in the Pensacola District. This job would be in addition to my regular shift work. My job was to train them on how to handle the many problems that can crop up during the course of a shift.

Soon after that Corporal James Hancock, who was my immediate supervisor and also the auxiliary supervisor, was taken off the auxiliary assignment and I became the supervisor. It became my job to set up schools and firearms training for new auxiliary men. This meant that I had to be sent to several schools where I became a certified police standards instructor and a state-certified firearms instructor.

When I became an instructor for teaching and firearms training, the FHP started using me to teach a few refresher classes at the FHP Academy and re-certify troopers in firearms training every six months. Along with my regular shift, I was becoming very busy with less and less free time to get into mischief.

One evening I was almost home myself when I heard Bob Newton call for assistance. He had picked up a car chase that had started in Santa Rosa County. Deputies were chasing the stolen car and couldn't catch it, so they called for assistance and Bob was the closest trooper to respond. He immediately called in and asked for a blocking trooper. I turned around, and taking every shortcut I could think of, I headed toward Bob. The chase was headed north on US Route 29 toward the state line about forty-five to fifty miles.

I came out on US Route 29, about a mile behind Bob, and was gaining with each mile. I approached a construction area where the two-lane road was being expanded to a four-lane road. A temporary lane had been made to move traffic from the old section to the new section, and this was where I got behind one of the slower deputy sheriff cars from Santa Rosa County. I was traveling about 135 miles per hour and had set up to pass the deputy as we came out of the crossover. At those speeds a person does not do a lot of looking in the rearview mirror, and I doubt the deputy even knew I was that close behind him. There was a southbound car approaching and the deputy, not being familiar with the road configuration, hit his brakes. There was very little room for me to maneuver away from him, so I took the only other option available to me: I hit the shoulder of the road, and since the grass was wet with dew, I started a sideways skid.

Had I stayed on the shoulder, I may have regained control of the car, but it started sliding back toward the pavement, which was the exact wrong thing to do. The car was loose in the grass on the shoulder and started to turn sideways as it slid. When the car returned to the pavement, it started overturning. The car overturned several times back onto the southbound shoulder of the road where it came to rest on its top.

I was still in my seatbelts behind the wheel and was looking out the windshield when the car came to a stop. Since it was dark and I was disoriented from the rollover, I had no idea where I was or what had happened. I unfastened my seat-belt to get out of the car. I immediately fell on my head onto the roof of the car. It was then that I realized that I was upside down and the chase was over for me. Just before the accident, I was within about three to five hundred feet of catching Bob and the car he was chasing.

I called for a supervisor, and they completed their investigation and took me home since I was not injured. As I went in the house, Vera asked me where I had wrecked. I asked if someone had called her and she answered no. She always seemed to know when I had been in an accident.

I had the opportunity to have my dad ride with me in 1976. That evening with my dad was one of my fondest memories. He was amazed at the "gadgets" we used to help us do our work. It was fun having him ride with me while we enjoyed each others company. He died about a year later in 1977 from a series of heart attacks, but I will always have that memory of the time we had that evening.

In 1979 I was promoted to Trooper II and became a traffic homicide investigator. I had gone to Bradenton, Florida, for an auxiliary conference and at the end of the conference was asked by the Troop A troop commander if I would drive him to Tallahassee, as his plane was grounded. On that trip he asked me if I would consider a Trooper II position in Pensacola if one became available. About a month later I received a letter of promotion. This was a godsend for Vera and me, since we were still financially struggling. The state legislature gave us a 9.5 percent merit pay raise that year and the promotion meant another 10 percent pay raise. So, the 19.5 percent pay raise all at once finally got our heads above the water for the first time in eleven years.

Trooper Bob Newton was my field training officer for my probationary period for the traffic homicide position. He had to take extra traffic fatalities so I could get in the required training. He was a good investigator and taught me a lot. The first fatality he let me work was a single-car accident where the driver was traveling too fast around a curve, ran off the road, and overturned.

These are the easiest of all accidents to investigate as a traffic homicide investigator since it is just a matter of reporting the cause of death and there is no court appearance required. I had worked many fatalities prior to this but not from the viewpoint of a traffic homicide investigator; this was exactly what I needed to start my career in a new field. I spent three months following Bob around and doing work he had to sign off on when I completed the report.

Finally I had found the position I had been looking for since I joined the FHP. I remained an investigator from then until I retired in 1989. My skills as a traffic homicide investigator were becoming well known throughout the patrol, and I started receiving calls from other investigators across the state, assisting them over the phone, interpreting their evidence, and helping them reach a conclusion as to what happened.

I taught accident investigation a few times at the FHP Academy and at the Law Enforcement School at Pensacola Junior College. I also taught defensive driving several nights a week. And about once a year, I set the curriculum and arranged instructors for the highway patrol auxiliary schools. These schools were for auxiliary men and women in Escambia, Santa Rosa, and Okaloosa counties. There were three instructor troopers, one for each county, and we all participated in putting on the classes. My own time to practice my craft was becoming very precious to me. It seemed like I was chasing my tail sometimes.

Late in 1979 the Liberty City riots started in Miami, when members of the city police department were accused of beating a black motorcyclist to death. They were later acquitted, causing the Liberty City section of Miami to erupt in riots. The city of Miami called the state for assistance. The FHP sent Troop A , the seventeen-man riot squad, plus three additional men to Dade County, along with the riot squads from the other troops throughout the state. I was one of the three additional men sent from Pensacola.

Since we traveled the farthest, we were last to arrive and got the midnight shift. I was assigned to ride with a Dade County deputy. We pretty much patrolled the entire riot area. I had my homicide camera with me, and I took lots of pictures of burned-out buildings and the men we were working with.

The next day, at the end of our shift, the deputy had court, so I had to call for a ride. Since everyone else had already finished their shifts, it was up to the shift sergeant to pick me up. One of the Dade County FHP sergeants came to get me and was upset because he thought I should have stayed with my shift of troopers. Then when he saw the camera I was carrying, he gave me a serious chewing out. He let me know that I was not a tourist down there to take pictures; I was there to work. He relented some when he realized that I had been assigned to the deputy, but he focused on the camera and said that I was to never bring it with me again. Since it was my FHP camera I used for investigations, that was hard to do. The next night I brought my personal camera, which was smaller and would fit in my pocket.

We stayed in Miami for about two weeks, cleaning up the mess and getting things back to normal. Our unit of twenty or so men returned to Troop A and resumed the regular work schedule. Later I was contacted by general headquarters about the pictures I had taken in Miami. They were wanting photos from anyone who had taken pictures for additional documentation.

Later that same year general headquarters used more of my photographs to document the FHP activity in the aftermath of Hurricane Frederick, which came ashore in the Pensacola area. I think the eye of the storm actually came ashore about sixty or so miles west of Pensacola, but we ended up with winds of over one hundred miles per hour.

Our shift was working the evening shift, so we rode out the storm in our patrol cars. Mostly we drove from one trooper's house to another, spotlighting them to check for damage and checking in on each other. I had Auxiliary Trooper Tommy Dean riding with me.

During the course of the night Adrian's Barbecue Restaurant remained the only place open. Gulf Power had set up generators there so their crews would have a place to go for food and coffee throughout the night. We used it for the same purposes.

On one foray checking the roads, Dean and I were traveling south on Mobile Highway near Michigan Avenue. On the corner was a Winn-Dixie grocery store. As we passed, with the wind howling, a portion of the roof came off and went airborne over the top of my car. Tommy turned white as a ghost and asked me to stop the car, which I did immediately. He opened the car door, leaned out, and threw up. He was that scared. Somehow we survived the night. About daylight we were released to go home, change into clean uniforms, and meet in a few hours at the station.

At the station we were met by several state representatives who wanted to see firsthand the storm damage. Our five-patrol car convoy left the station, with each of us carrying a couple of representatives. We went out to Pensacola Beach and surveyed the damage there. One of the cars bogged down in the drifted sand, so we all got out and pushed it free. We also went to Gulf Beach Highway, where there was severe damage to an entire subdivision. Then we were instructed to go out to NAS Sherman Field at the navy base, as President Jimmy Carter would be flying in after surveying the area damage in Alabama and Florida.

When we arrived, I had Senator Tom Tobiassen with me. He was instructed to proceed to the reception line area, near where the president's helicopter was to land, and all of us troopers were to remain in the building. This move aggravated me since I had worked during the entire storm event and now I was not going to get to meet the president of the United States, and others that had been safe at home during the storm were.

As time grew near for the president to arrive, I grabbed a tray with water and headed out to Senator Tobiassen. I quietly told him why I was there and that the water was a ruse. He told me it was too late to return to the hangar where we were staying since the helicopter was already landing. Senator Tobiassen had me stand beside him in the reception line. President Jimmy Carter walked along the line, and each person was supposed to introduce themselves and announce their job, and then get their photo taken with the president.

When it came our turn, Senator Tobiassen gently nudged me out front, where I shook hands with President Carter. He asked my job, to which I replied that I was a road trooper and had worked all night during the storm. He paused then asked how my family had fared without me. I told him, he wished me well, and we had our photo taken together shaking hands. I later went to the newspaper to get a copy of the photo and noticed that, out of all the pictures I saw, mine was the only one in which both parties were facing the camera. Several years later I sent a copy of the picture to Plains, Georgia, and he signed it and returned the photo. That was a good memory.

One evening I clocked a Pontiac Trans-Am and a Corvette racing at a high rate of speed. They had no idea that I was anywhere close. I followed them to the Pine Forest Road exit, where a well-known barbecue restaurant was located. They pulled into the lot with me right behind them.

I told the drivers that I was issuing citations, and one driver laughed and said, "Officer, I'm going to give you one more chance to change your mind." Of course I didn't and after the paperwork was finished, I left.

Several years later I was with a bunch of Tate High School band boosters at a local eatery and they were discussing tickets they had received, not knowing I was a trooper. One was talking about getting a ticket for speeding on I-10 one evening while racing with another car. I let him tell the whole story before revealing that I was the trooper who had written those citations. We had a good laugh and are still friends.

Our boys were members of the Tate High School band, so we joined the band boosters. I became president of the band boosters and remained president for three years. Vera and I were chaperones on every trip the band took, from Friday football games to band contests across the southeast. Vera and I were so involved in their school activities that those four years seemed to fly by.

One of the last trips we took with the band was to Miami, where the band marched in the Orange Bowl Parade and participated in the Orange Bowl Band contest. The band was large so we traveled in six chartered buses with an instrument truck following along behind. On the first evening in Miami, the bus drivers decided we needed to dump the holding tanks in the buses and started to the dumping center in North Miami. The road took them through Liberty City, where I had been during the Liberty City riots in 1980.

I was driving the instrument truck with two other boosters along with me. As we passed places that I recognized, I would tell them of people being killed at this intersection or that one. During a lull I turned the switch off and back on, making the truck backfire. The next thing I knew, both men were hiding on the floor of the truck!

As my sons, Kent and Kelly, got a little older, they showed interest in riding with me on weekends and during the summer when they were out of school. We had some good times together, and they learned firsthand what happened when drinking and driving. I did not shield them from the accidents or from going inside the jail when I took in prisoners. I also took them into emergency rooms to see the injured and maimed. It did make an impression on them and they are better for the experience.

Kelly was riding with me one evening when we were working traffic on I-110. I clocked a motorcycle at a fairly high rate of speed and turned around to pursue. The driver saw me turn and started evasive action. He was trying to outrun me. I called for backup and started overtaking the motorcycle. The driver turned off I-110 onto Brent Lane, onto Davis Highway, and then turned south toward the neighborhoods.

Unfortunately, the driver must not have been familiar with the area he was in because he turned back west where all the roads ended at the interstate fence. He then turned into a trailer park with me right behind and crowding him. He finally stopped, jumped off the motorcycle, ran to the nearest trailer, and went inside without knocking. I followed him inside and found him trying to crawl under a bed. The owner of the trailer did not know the running driver and said that he had tried to go out the back door but found it locked. All this time, Kelly was excited and amazed that we had actually stayed with the motorcycle around curves, over speed bumps, and along the narrow streets.

Kent saw what happened when drinking and driving resulted in accidents. He was with me when I pulled a drunk out of his car after he had run off into a ditch. He was so drunk that he had soiled himself and couldn't remember his own name or where he was. Kent also saw how drunk drivers were treated at the county jail. They were not mistreated, but they lost their right to go where they wanted to go.

I always cautioned both Kent and Kelly that what happened in my car stayed in my car. They were never to talk with their mom or their friends about what they saw or heard while they were riding with me. That was a strict rule I had with anyone who rode with me, especially my sons.

One evening the FHP was notified of a pedestrian being struck on Old Palafox Highway in the Ensley community. Trooper Tommy Langston was dispatched, and since I was the homicide investigator on call, I also responded in case I was needed. If not needed, I would assist with traffic.

Trooper Langston and I arrived about the same time and found a crowd of about fifty people and a car in the ditch with a man under the right front tire. As we approached the vehicle, the man could be seen and was clearly dead, since the tire was sitting on his head. However, there were bubbles coming out his nose, so it was necessary to check for a pulse, which Trooper Langston did.

Someone in the crowd said, "Ooh, dat man bees alive! You gots to give him mouth-to-mouth resuckitation." I looked at Trooper Langston and told him that, since I was the homicide investigator, that would be his job.

Trooper Langston leaned over the dead man and said, "Ooh, dat man bees dead!" That satisfied the crowd until the ambulance arrived. They got the dead man out from under the car and the crowd realized that he was indeed dead when they covered him with a sheet.

In another incident I investigated, a man was injured when he jumped from a moving vehicle while driving on I-10. He said that he went home after being out drinking with friends, and he and his wife became embroiled in a huge fight. His two small children became scared with all the screaming and yelling so they went outside and crawled into the rear seat of the family car.

As the fight raged on, the driver decided he'd had enough, so he ran out, jumped in the car, and left. As he was driving along the interstate, he heard a noise in the backseat of the car. He reached over the seat and felt a head. Fearing that he was about to be attacked, he jumped out of the moving car. He had no idea that he had left his two sons to their fate in the still-moving car. The now driver-less car continued along the interstate, slowing and drifting onto the shoulder of the road, where it struck a pine tree. Thankfully the children were sitting in the floor of the rear seat when the car collided with the tree and received minor injuries. Needless to say, the driver was cited for reckless driving and reckless endangerment of the children.

I was called out to conduct a traffic homicide investigation late one night. The accident had occurred on I-110 north of Brent Lane. In it a speeding motorcyclist crashed into the rear of a slower-moving semi-trailer. The driver of the motorcycle was killed in the crash.

It became the duty of Trooper Rick Crinshaw to notify the next of kin regarding the death of the driver. Rick came to me and asked if I would accompany him to the house for the notification, as he was uncomfortable doing that duty alone.

We located the house well back in a neighborhood at about 3:30 a.m. The woman who answered the door had been aroused from her sleep and was confused due to the hour, plus she could barely speak broken English. We tried to tell her about her husband's death to no avail. She finally let us know she had a priest that could speak Spanish and we placed the call. He said he would be out as soon as he was able.

In the meantime we sat in the living room with the lights down low, and Rick and I talked about the investigation. Suddenly, over in a corner of the room, a parrot that we did not know about woke up and let out an extremely loud squawk. Rick, who was already jumpy due to the circumstances, ran for the front screen door. He had no idea what was causing that racket and never slowed down when he hit the screen. He went out into the yard, dragging the remains of the screen door behind him. I looked out the door and there was Rick with his gun out and pointed back at the house. I was laughing so hard I had tears, and the lady, who was trying to be upset because she had two police officers in her home, was also laughing because of what her bird had caused. Notifying the next of kin in a fatal accident was part of our duty, but sometimes even the most difficult duties could have a humorous side to them.

I was working the midnight shift when another trooper received a call of an accident on the Escambia River Bridge on US Route 90. I responded and offered assistance since it was on a bridge. The road had four lanes and was divided by a grassy median until the bridges. There were two bridges that were elevated across the river to allow barge traffic to pass underneath. The accident occurred on the westbound bridge. The land under the bridge fell away pretty fast and there was quite a drop to the ground before the river was crossed. As we were working the accident, a helpful motorist stopped on the east bridge and called out that he was trained in first aid and would come over and assist.

Before anyone could stop him, the helper leaped over the railing, thinking that it was simply a divider. He fell about eighteen feet to the ground under the bridge. We knew it was about to get worse for him since he screamed all the way to the ground. I don't remember whether he ended up with just one leg broken or both of them.

My sons learned early that I could pull a practical joke on anyone at any time. I suspect that Kelly had been on the butt end of one of my jokes a time or two, which led to the following story. He knew that I was jumpy and didn't sleep well at night and would get up at any slight noise and check the house. That, by the way, was a byproduct of being a policeman. I often still do that at night all these years later.

Kelly had a job working as a clerk at a store that rented VHS movies. Some of the advertisements for movies were often full-sized cardboard cutouts of the star of the movie. Kelly brought one of them home one night after work and propped it up in the kitchen near the breakfast bar. He knew I would hear him come home and spoke to me before going to his room. Later he made a small noise outside his room that he knew I would react to and waited. I got up and looked out my bedroom door down the hallway toward the kitchen and saw a silhouette.

I was armed and asked who was there and started down the hall. I received no response; the silhouette just stood there.

I said, "You better speak up or pay the price!" By this time I was close enough that I saw it was one of his cutouts and I must have let out a groan. As I passed Kelly's room, headed back to bed, I heard a small chuckle and knew he had got me.

In October every year St. Ann's Catholic Church in Pensacola held a fall festival. In a pecan orchard on the church grounds, they had built a replica of an old Western town. They had food booths, carnival games, and several different types of events, which included local school bands, cowboy "shoot-outs," and TV celebrities. These events lasted for three days and they hired the FHP auxiliary as the security. As supervisor of the auxiliary, I became the head of the security detail. I generally was there from the time it opened until the bank run was made at the end of each night. During my eleven years with the FHPA, I met lots of celebrities and was charged with being their bodyguard while they were on church grounds.

John Schneider, star of the TV series *The Dukes of Hazard*, was one of the biggest celebrities I had to deal with at St. Ann's. The crowd was upward of sixty thousand people, all of whom were trying to see or touch the celebrity. Touching in that kind of crowd meant grabbing, which I could not allow. As we headed to the rear of the main building, where we were to exit the area, we were met by the biggest crowd I had ever seen, short of the crowd in Miami in 1972. I had a security person park my car crossways to the alley, and we actually had to be pulled across the hood of my car to avoid the crowd.

Several years later Mr. Schneider returned to Pensacola to the interstate fairgrounds where he was to sing. I met him again and we had a few minutes to reminisce about his first visit. He was and is a nice man.

All the celebrities I met were afraid of crowds. I suspect that was their biggest fear. All wanted to sign autographs and shake hands with people but needed to feel safe when doing so. None would venture outside our security ring unless I was personally with them.

About three weeks after the St. Ann's festival, the Pensacola Interstate Fair started. It lasted for seven to ten days. The FHPA was also their security detail, so I was out there for most of the time it was open. About the only thing that took me away from the fair was my rotation for a traffic homicide.

One evening at the fair a deputy asked me to go with him as his backup to one of the beer gardens on the grounds. He had been called to a disturbance there. At the beer garden we encountered several people fighting. As we tried to separate them, an extremely obese woman stumbled, accidentally knocked me down, and fell on top of me, breaking three of my ribs.

In 1980 Fidel Castro released hundreds of criminals from his prisons in Cuba and sent them to the United States. This move became known as the Mariel Boat Lift, since most had to be rescued from the ocean by our Coast Guard. They eventually ended up in Miami, where they wreaked all kinds of havoc. The Miami police department was overwhelmed with criminal activity caused by these Cubans and asked for help from the state.

The governor of Florida at the time was Bob Graham, who was himself a resident of the Miami area. Governor Graham asked that one hundred state troopers be reassigned to Miami to handle the routine police work while the Miami police handled the crimes being committed. The FHP selected the troopers and started a rotation of troopers going down to Dade County for the next six months. I was reassigned in the second rotation and became a city police officer in the city of Miami for three months.

The city was so appreciative that they enlisted the entire business community to assist them in making our life a little easier, since we were being dragged away from our families for such a long period. The hotels gave us rooms at no charge and the restaurants fed us twice a day at no charge. Dry cleaners, repair shops, and other services were knocking themselves out to make our stay a little better.

The state paid us our standard per diem rate and we were allowed to work seven days a week while we were on detail. This allowed the state to pay us sixteen hours a week overtime, and on top of that, the city allowed those of us assigned to the city police department to work off-duty employment another eight hours a day at the going rate. All this meant was that I was making about twice my normal pay and did not have to spend any of it to live on down there.

About three weeks into the detail, I called Vera and asked if she would come down for the weekend. She had no idea what I was doing, and since she felt we couldn't afford it, she said she would catch a bus and come down. I told her how much money I had accumulated working the off-duty jobs and that we could easily afford a plane ticket. She flew down and spent the weekend with me. The car rental agency supplied us a car at no expense and every restaurant we went to offered us a bottle of wine with our meal. That was an enjoyable weekend getaway for us. While she was there, I did not have to give up the overtime but did suspend the off-duty work for those days.

One of the off-duty jobs I was sent out on was guarding a warehouse being renovated in the Overtown area of Miami. This was one of the areas where riots had taken place the year before and it was really a dangerous part of the city. That night I was sitting in my unit, watching the fence line, when a man on a motorcycle drove up. He asked if I wanted to purchase an Uzi. Being from the rural, north part of the state, I had never encountered this kind of thing before. I said no and he handed me a business card; on it was the name of "The Turk" and a phone number. He said if I changed my mind, to give him a call.

The dispatchers with the city also had their fun with us. The Miami police would get weird calls, as we all did from time to time, but their fun came in sending their rookies on these calls. I chased blind calls to check out nude women on balconies in condo units to unknown persons trying to steal a city bus. I was even assigned to the area in and around Little Havana.

I enjoyed the handrolled cigars and the Cuban coffee. As a state trooper we never left our cars for foot patrols since we didn't have hand-held radios, but when we arrived in Miami they issued us the hand-held units. I actually liked to walk foot patrol and meet people and visit with them. They could tell I was one of the special detail troopers since I had a real southern accent. Those folks seemed to enjoy my southern drawl as much as I enjoyed the Spanish I was hearing.

In Pensacola when an accident occurred, the occupants of the wrecked cars stayed put until a trooper arrived to handle the paperwork. In Miami I would get a call of an accident, but generally by the time I arrived, there was nothing left but a pile of glass. I did work about 150 accidents the first month I was there and wrote over 300 citations during the same period. That was the most of both I had ever written in a thirty-day period.

The first couple of weeks in Miami I had a roommate from Baldwin, Florida. One afternoon I was called to the station and advised that my roommate's best friend, another trooper, had been shot and killed back in Baldwin.

It became my responsibility to tell him of the death and get him started back home.

My tour in Miami was supposed to be for ninety days but was cut short when I was reassigned to homicide school in Tallahassee. I had time enough to drive the seven hundred miles home, kiss the wife, repack my bags, and head to Tallahassee. All in all my time as a city policeman was a good time. I also made enough money on that detail to build a shop I had been wanting behind our house. For our effort of going to Miami as city policemen, we were acknowledged by the state legislature for the sacrifice.

Several months later I was summoned back to court in Dade County, regarding some of the citations I had written while I was down there. In Pensacola things tended to be a great deal slower in court than was the case in the Dade County court system. I was assigned four sessions in court with about twenty cases per session. I noted on the subpoena that thirty minutes had been allotted for each session.

I was directed by the department to catch the early flight from Pensacola to Miami, and I would be met by the court liaison trooper who would provide transportation to court. I was met by one of the Pensacola troopers still assigned to the Mariel detail. By the time I finally got to the correct court room, the first session was over and the court room was empty.

The rest of my allotted sessions went off without a hitch, and they were interesting. The very first question the judge asked was, "Does anyone want to change their plea?" The first question from the judge to me was, "Were you a witness to any of the accidents you investigated?"

The next question to the audience was, "Are there any other witnesses to this accident?" He then either tried the case or dismissed the case, depending on whether a witness showed up. It didn't take long for the court room to empty. We were finished in less than the thirty minutes allotted to my cases.

In 1982 I returned to Miami for the third time in three years for a special detail. President Ronald Reagan was to meet Pope John Paul II there for two or three days of meetings. We had to get down there about a week prior to their visit. We had our own meetings and worked out details of our part in the event. The FHP was assigned all the expressways, and on the day of the event, when the president and the pope were using the roads, nothing was to be on them. We had assigned places we were to park, and we were not to be on the road ourselves when the motorcades were moving.

I was again assigned a familiar sergeant on this detail. He had a long memory from the time I was down in Miami for the Liberty City riots. The same sergeant who chastised me for having a camera with me during work hours, assigned me to the toll plaza on the Airport Expressway. It would be my job to get all the employees of the toll booth inside the main plaza building and keep them there until the presidential detail passed. He vaguely implied that I should be inside the building with them. I took that as a maybe as long as I saw that the toll collectors were inside.

On the day of the event we started clearing the expressway routes and called wreckers for stalled or abandoned vehicles. I saw a semi truck trailer wrecker for the first time when I called for a wrecker for a stalled city bus. The bus was loaded up on the trailer in about five minutes and was gone. With the expressways clear, I headed for my assigned position. About an hour later I received word that the motorcade was headed my way, so I moved all the toll takers into the main building. I remained outside the door and was in that position when President Reagan and Mrs. Reagan slowed and were driven through the toll booth. I received a smile and a wave from them both.

Back in Pensacola it was back to the usual routine and more traffic fatalities. At a place near McDavid, Florida, the owner of a local dairy was traveling south on US Route 29 when his car had a blowout. The car swerved and struck a bridge abutment, ejecting the driver, who was killed. I was up at the accident site the next day and had taken additional measurements and more photographs of the scene. I had just retrieved my camera equipment from the trunk of my car and was closing the trunk lid when a large gravel truck came by. As it passed, a rock fell from the truck and struck me in the eye. I wear glasses, so the rock actually struck them and broke the lens. Fortunately I was not injured and immediately called the shift supervisor and advised him what had happened.

From our conversation, I gathered that he did not want to make the trip all the way out to where I was and asked me to meet him at a location closer to town. I reminded him that my glasses were broken, and after a long pause, he said I should stay put and he would come to me. He brought an auxiliary man along with him who drove my car back to the station.

There was another fatal accident on a county road in Santa Rosa County in a farming community. I arrived on the scene and found a car sitting out in a field, with the left door open and the engine still running. A pedestrian lying in the roadway near the car was the fatality.

At first glance it appeared that the driver of the car had struck and killed the pedestrian and then fled the scene. The car had come to a stop in a plowed field, so the tracks showed how the car traveled from the road to its final location. However, I could not see any tracks from the driver leaving the car.

I found out the car belonged to the pedestrian, and after talking to a local farmer who was working his field about a quarter mile away, I was able to determine what happened. The pedestrian was a local woman who drove around the back roads and would stop when she saw an aluminum can or a glass soda bottle; she would pick them up for resale. According to the farmer, he saw her car stop, and the next time he saw it, the car was in the field with the door open. After it did not move for a while, he became curious and went to investigate. He found the pedestrian and called the FHP.

Based on the evidence, it appeared that the driver stopped when she saw an aluminum can in the road. Rather than exit the car, she stopped, and with her foot on the brake and her hand on the steering wheel, she leaned out the open car door and tried to retrieve the can. When she leaned out she lost her balance and fell out. The car, still in gear, started rolling and ran over the woman as she lay on the road. She was both the driver and the pedestrian and was listed as such on the traffic homicide report. That caused some confusion for the reviewing supervisor, but after lengthy discussions, neither the supervisor nor I could figure any other way to list her on the report.

Another bizarre accident I investigated happened on a foggy night on I-10. I was called out to investigate a fatality north of Pensacola. When I arrived I noted the remains of possibly the most damaged vehicle I had ever investigated. It was sitting in the median and looked like someone dropped a pile of junk there. A closer investigation showed duel tire tracks from a semi, either the truck or the trailer, going right over the driver's seat. The nude body of the lone occupant was in several pieces around the car. There was a truck sitting on the shoulder about four hundred feet east of the car. The investigating trooper told me that from the truck driver's statement, the car came out of the fog so close that he hardly had time to hit his brakes before he hit the car head-on.

What made this accident so bizarre was that the driver of the car was nude. There was one spot in the remains of the car that was less damaged than the rest. In the right front floor I located neatly folded clothes that belonged to the driver: shoes, socks, underwear, and outer clothing. There were no witnesses to the accident other than the truck driver, and the physical evidence I saw and located substantiated his statement.

In the driver's belongings were his ID and a plastic tab with a room key attached. Obviously the key was a motel room key, but there was no name on the tab. I located the motel and all I got from the clerk was that the deceased had checked in late—that was the last he was seen by anyone associated with the motel. Out of the skimpy evidence I had from the scene and from the driver's friends in Birmingham, I was able to piece together most of the story as to how this accident occurred.

The deceased had left Birmingham, Alabama, after work. He drove to Pensacola, arriving about 10:00 p.m. He left his motel room sometime after that and traveled to an unknown location. At some point in his travels he removed all his clothes, and due to the fog and being unfamiliar with the area, he drove onto the exit ramp at Scenic Highway and I-10. Blood levels indicated intoxication, so drinking became a factor also. He managed to drive just about a mile in the wrong lane before being struck and killed by the truck.

I speculated on several different theories about how the driver came to be where he was and nude, but I could never get a fact to agree with any of them.

Around 1985 I started traveling to Tallahassee about once every two months for a couple of weeks at a time to assist the coordinator of the traffic homicide division, Stu Akers, in catching up on reviewing every traffic homicide investigation statewide. Not only did this job bring satisfaction, but it also showed me what other investigators were doing and that I was able to get even better at my job.

In 1988 we traveled to Kansas to visit relatives. I met with the owners of A-Lert Corporation and was invited to join their growing construction company. They were having an unusual rash of industrial accidents and would soon be starting a safety department at the request of their insurance company. They thought that with my experience as an investigator and dealing with attorneys and insurance companies, I would be a good fit in their company. I traveled to Decatur, Illinois, with one of the owners to look over a job site where one of their employees had fallen and received severe injuries. On the return trip I advised him that I needed some time to think about such a move. I had not reached twenty-five years on the FHP yet, and although I was getting burned out on all the traffic deaths, I wasn't sure I was ready to quit. I also didn't know how it would affect my retirement.

We returned to Pensacola and I resumed my job. I had forgotten about the job offer when I received a call from one of the owners in the fall of that year. He said that they were about to hire someone for the safety job; they wanted it to be me but I had to decide. I had paid into the retirement account enough to cover the time I was in the military during war time, and I found that the combined time would give me twenty-five years retirement if I left in January 1989. I submitted my papers and pulled the pin, retiring from the Florida Highway Patrol as a traffic homicide investigator with the equivalent rank of sergeant.

PART IV:

Epilogue

God gives each of us a talent, and it is up to each person to develop and use that talent. My talent was traffic homicide investigations, reconstructing auto accidents where people were killed.

In January 1989, I started work as the risk manager with A-Lert Corporation in Fredonia, Kansas. As a state trooper I was used to having people listen when I spoke. In the private sector, especially the construction industry I was entering, I found that I was being questioned everywhere I spoke. It was the same question at each stop: "How can you tell us about safety when you have never worked in construction before?" My response was, "I am not going to try and tell you how to do your jobs, but I am going to give you information that will help you do them safely." As in any job, I had to earn the respect of the men that I was working with.

Working with the company insurance representatives helped me formulate a plan for the new safety department. After many interviews and open safety meetings at many job sites, I made recommendations to the company that eventually reduced their accidents and their insurance.

Vera and I bought a small ranch about ten miles west of Fredonia and called that home. On the ranch property I found an old wheel from some sort of farm implement.

When a state trooper dies in the State of Florida, we call it the "broken spoke," so it was natural that I name the ranch the Broken Wheel Ranch. But even that was not enough to keep us in Kansas. Although it was good being near both our families, Vera and I found that we both missed Florida.

So after a year and a half, I resigned and we returned to our home in Florida. Vera had insisted that we keep our house there because she knew that someday we would want to return, and I was glad she did.

Upon returning to Florida, I reapplied to the FHP for my old job. I found out that I was unable to rejoin the FHP due to my failing eye sight. I finally went to work for Sunshine Junior Foods in Panama City, Florida. There I worked as an internal theft investigator in the auditing department. I eventually worked my way up to director of internal audit.

I finally realized that my first love was working accidents and helping people, as I did when I was a state trooper. So, with some encouragement from my family, I started my own consulting business.

I went to the law firm of Kerrigan, Estess, Rankin, and McLeod and talked to my friend Bob Kerrigan, who hired me as a contract employee. He and one of his partners made sure that I had all the work I needed. They are a firm of very nice people and they helped me more than I could possibly describe. I will always be eternally grateful for what they did for me.

On one job, after looking at the police report and the traffic homicide investigation report, I concluded that the investigating officers got the reports all wrong and advised the attorney handling the case to save the victim's car, as it was the proof of the investigation being wrong.

During another case I investigated in Tampa, I interviewed the traffic homicide investigator and located the vehicle. The damage to the vehicle did not show that there was sufficient damage to cause fatal injuries. Further investigation revealed that the car manufacturer had installed the wrong steering column. The vehicle was supposed to have a collapsible column but instead had a solid column from an earlier model. The firm also purchased that vehicle for further analysis.

Eventually this led to me joining with retired Pensacola city policeman Brian Burton in forming an accident reconstruction company. Our primary job was to travel to an accident site for information and, along with the police report, reconstruct the accident for courtroom presentation. We also went to the University of North Florida in Jacksonville and were certified to obtain information from computers installed in motor vehicles and learned crash animation for courtroom presentation.

At the time, I was running with a small group of investigators that had befriended me when I first started my own agency. One of that group, Dick Danley, was not only an investigator for a local law firm but an ex-state trooper from Florida. Another was my friend with the same firm I was working for, Jim Horton. Over coffee one time I had told them of living in Independence, Kansas, the home of playwright William Inge. One of his Broadway plays, *Picnic*, was based loosely on an annual event in Independence called Neewollah. (That is

Halloween spelled backward.) It is a big event in this small southeast Kansas town.

Of course not only was the story not believed but they actually laughed about it. So I, being the type of guy I was, took their laughter in stride and decided it was time for a little payback. On one of our yearly visits to Kansas, I stopped in the Neewollah merchandise store for T-shirts. I also picked up a schedule of events for the week of the celebration. I had one of Vera's friends sign it and had her write that she was Queen Neelah, the queen of Neewollah. I gave both Danley and Horton a signed copy of the schedule, supposedly signed by the queen. Both had the signed schedule framed and hung them on the walls of their offices. I have not, until this writing, ever mentioned this to anyone. That was one of the best "gotchas" I ever did.

In 1999, I had a small heart attack. It was the type I never felt, but it required open heart surgery and three bypasses. After the heart attack I lost interest in the investigation business and had continuing health problems. I was in and out the hospital with chest pains over the next few years.

During that recovery period I had another close call. Working for the Florida Highway Patrol taught me certain skills in driving techniques. This came in handy one afternoon when Vera and I were going into town on an errand. As I topped a hill, I noticed a car in the oncoming lane had stopped in the road to allow a child pushing a bicycle to cross the highway in front of his car. I was almost on top of this incident by the time I registered what was happening. When the child saw my car, he stopped right in the middle of my lane. I realized that I would not be able to stop in time to avoid hitting him.

My vehicle was equipped with anti-lock brakes, thank God, and I was able to hit the brakes and maintain control of the vehicle. I opted to swerve onto the shoulder and thereby avoid the child. But as I turned toward the shoulder, I saw a second child standing on the edge of the road in a narrow driveway, waiting for the boy with the bicycle. Time seemed to slow down. I locked eyes with the second child and willed him to stand still. Had he moved, I would have hit him. I managed to miss the boy on the shoulder by fractions of an inch. I crossed the driveway where the child was standing and continued on through underbrush and back onto the shoulder, where I bounced over a dead pine tree that was lying on the shoulder. When the car came to a stop, we were uninjured and the child had run home. There was virtually no damage to my car.

In 2004, Hurricane Ivan struck, and our home received extreme damage from a tree that fell through the roof of the house. A few days later I suffered another serious bout with my heart. I believe that was the second minor heart attack I suffered.

In 2006, after yet another episode of chest pains, one of my cardiologists told me that they had located another blockage that was causing all the pain. It was their decision that I could have a heart attack there and it wouldn't be fatal. It wasn't their heart or their decision to make as far as I was concerned. After arguing with them, I went back to my friend Bob Kerrigan and told him what was happening. He was furious that the cardiologist was willing for me to have a heart attack at all. At first he wanted to send me to the Mayo Clinic in Minnesota, but his partner, George Estess, knew one of the cardiologists in the group I was going to and called him. After the call they relented and decided that they could do something about the recurring chest pains I was having. I finally received a stint.

Since that day in 2006, I have not suffered any kind of chest pain and have returned to a productive life. After seven years of chest pains, I felt like it was the first day of the rest of my life.

When I turned sixty-two, I finally said I'd had enough and retired for good. I knew that with heart disease, tomorrow is not guaranteed, nor is it with anyone else, so we started traveling more to see the country.

From being a "dirty little Indian kid," which someone once called me when I was growing up in Oklahoma, to having a successful career as a state trooper and consultant, it has been one heck of a ride. It has been a ride that I have finally come to realize I could not have made without a good woman beside me and my belief in God.

It is my hope that I can interview other retired troopers and tell their stories before it is too late. Many of my friends, some mentioned in these pages, that I have worked with over the years in Pensacola, Tallahassee, and Cocoa are starting to die off.

Soon it will be my turn to once again be young and drive those rockets that we called highway patrol cars. It truly does take a young man to be a state trooper, and I hope God needs us in heaven so I can once again feel the exhilaration of driving fast.

Well, that's my story. The end has yet to be written, but as I have said before, it has been quite a ride. There are many, many stories that will never reach the light of day, and they should not because they have no place in this narrative. They are part of the past and should not be resurrected. They are those things that are only talked about with another trooper over a cup of coffee or at the end of a shift.

May God smile down on you and may your road always be smooth and straight.

About the Author

Tom Verge retired from the Florida Highway Patrol after serving twenty-one years as a road trooper and traffic homicide investigator. He lives in Pensacola, Florida, with his wife, Vera. He has two sons and four grandchildren. Tom is an active deacon at his church and does volunteer work at the local veterans' clinic. This book, *After Roll Call*, is the memoir of his time on the Florida Highway Patrol. He has plans to write another book of additional highway patrol stories.